Rock and Roses

An Anthology of Mountaineering Essays

Edited by Mikel Vause, Ph.D.

Published by Mountain N'Air Books

ISBN: 1-879415-01-1

Table of Contents

Introduction

People need to participate in adventure, to pioneer new frontiers, sometimes even at the risk of life, and to do it under their own power using few or possibly none of technology's products to add an even greater feeling of accomplishment and contribute to their ascent--physically and spiritually.

When one thinks of mountaineering, generally it is in the masculine sense, and in the past men were mostly responsible for the advances made in the sport. But today things have changed. Women have taken an active role in the development of new and difficult routes in all of the major mountain ranges of the world.

The essays contained in this collection are those of women. Women bold enough to break the old ideological mode set for them by society and to go seeking adventure. The writings herein approach climbing with the same poetic enthusiasm as the scholar climbers of the "Golden Age."

Rather than mere journalistic reports of climbs that are filled with unimaginative route and equipment descriptions, the reader finds stimulating philosophical treatments of universal issues with climbing as the central focus. Each essay in this compilation draws the reader into an active participation with its author whether it be responding to the death of a friend or family member as in the works of Linda Givler, and Julie Brugger or the pressures of being a lone woman on an all male climb, as with the essays by Arlene Blum and Alison Osius. In some of the essays, the reader is confronted with logistical problems that are inherent with climbing, particularly those of an expedition leader, as in Post Card, by Sue Giller. Other of the essays deal with the history of women's climbing and with the history comes an appreciation for the obstacles women had to face and overcome in an endeavor that has, with few exceptions, been dominated by men, as is clear when reading Ruth Dyar Mendenhall, Laura Waterman and Betty Woolsey.

From a literary standpoint, about the best compliment an author can receive from a reader is to find that the reader actively participated with the author while reading. Each of the essays mentioned here and all those others in this collection represent the kind of literature that pulls the reader in, forcing involvement in much the same way climbing does.

The contributors come from vast and varied backgrounds, everything from climbing guides to journalists and scientists. But what is most exciting about this collection is that it represents the innermost thoughts and feelings of women from vastly different backgrounds that are strung together by a common element: climbing mountains.

Mikel Vause

No Spare Rib
The Advent of Hard Women Rock Climbers

Rosie Andrews

"I have long believed that physical fitness is the key to woman's emancipation. All over the country women are loosening their girdles, and tightening their abdomens."

Olga Connolly, Olympic Gold-Medalist, Discus, 1956.

While rock climbing has always been male-dominated, in the past ten years the involvement of women has increased dramatically. The achievements of the most dedicated and talented women climbers indicate that in rock climbing women have found a sport in which equal status is well within reach. An article published recently in a British climbing magazine stated that women in the U.K. are currently climbing at a standard set by men twenty years ago. Probably this statement is more a reflection of ignorance of women's actual achievements than truth. Generally only those who choose to be vocal about thier accomplishments gain recognition for them. Certainly it is far from true in the U.S. While men continue to push the limits of the sport, women are making great strides towards closing the gap.

For men raised in a traditional western culture, learning to lead requires the application of skills closely related to his male heritage. While he may never have seen climbing hardware or have been aware that people climb rock faces, he has generally been encouraged to perform physically, problem-solve, take risks, compete, and learn to rely on himself. These aspects of male socialization provide a foundation which helps instill confidence as he enters into a new, risk-laden sport. Obviously not every western male has had an identical upbringing, but these are traits which are generally fostered and respected in the major institutions where socialization takes place.

Women, on the other hand, have been groomed for a very different role. Girls are usually more sheltered and protected, with little emphasis on risk taking. Rather than being prepared for independence, we learn to expect to play a supporting role which hinges upon reliance on others. Physically active little girls often earn the label "tomboy," and are encouraged to participate in more feminine activities. Thus, for many women, excelling in a sport like rock climbing means going against the grain of social experience, and learning to overcome obstacles created by growing up female.

When I began to climb regularly, in 1978, there were very few other women climbers in the north-eastern United States. As a result, I began to develop a reputation as a good "woman" climber, while leading at a standard long since surpassed by men, about 5.8 to 5.9. While the attention was somewhat flattering, there seemed to me to be a flaw inherent in my receiving recognition for something so unremarkable in terms of what was taking place in the sport. The overall impression was that I was doing something remarkable, "for a woman. " News travelled of women climbing at a much higher standard in other parts of the country: Coral Bowman was doing difficult 5.11 leads in Colorado and elsewhere. Beverly Johnson soloed El Cap's Dihedral Wall, but they were mythical Western figures, unseen in the more provincial world of Eastern climbing. Barbara Devine was perhaps the best known woman who had done hard climbs in the East, but she had relocated in the Midwest.

Six years later, the picture has changed considerably. Female climbing teams are no longer an unusual sight. While women remain well outnumbered by male climbers, those who are good have gained the respect of the climbing community on a more equal basis. At times there have been four or five women climbing at the Shawangunks, all of whom lead 5.11 or better. In all major U.S. areas, women have established themselves solidly in the 5.11 grade, and a few outstanding climbers have come far closer to the top of the scale. Visiting Australian climber Louise Shepherd's list of accomplishments included difficult routes in excellent style at many major areas when she toured the Western U.S. in 1982. Among her noteworthy ascents were the Yosemite climbs Tales of Power (5.12b, 1 fall), Separate Reality (5.12b, no falls), and Crimson Cringe (5.12a, 1 fall). Californian Lynn Hill has helped to establish a different perception of women in climbing through her impact on the sport. While attending college in New Paltz, where the Shawangunks are located, she had done many of the area's hardest climbs, including Supercrack (5.13) and Vandals

(5.12). The fact that Lynn has only climbed sporadically over the past two years makes these ascents even more impressive.

The beauty of climbing lies in the variety of skills it requries, and the unique way in which each climb draws upon those skills. The top-level climber exhibits physical and psychological control through movement, problem-solving, and maintaining composure under pressure. Because each climb is different, there is no single key to top performance. There is simply a grade, within which many climbs exist, each of which demands varying degrees of strength, technical skill, and commitment. This lack of constants plays a large role in keeping climbing interesting, since failure or success on one climb is no guarantee of similar results on the next. It is also a factor which favors women's participation, since specific features of body type can be as much an advantage as a disadvantage. For example, while women are often hampered by a lack of reach, we also tend to have smaller hands and fingers, a definite aid on thin cracks or small face holds. Thus a natural balancing exists which is lacking in many sports which emphasize traits such as large size, where men have the obvious advantage.

An accurate portrayal of women's participation in rock climbing today is to consider the two major elements of the sport separately. Do women have the potential physical ability to climb the hardest route, and do women have the psychological strength to actualize their physical potential?

The physical portion of this inquiry is more easily addressed. In general, differences in athletic performance between men and women are due to differences in body size and composition. The capacities of the energy systems of the female are less than those of the male, and the absolute strength (power) of females is about two-thirds that of males. Physiology has a tremendous impact on women's performance in sports such as running, basketball, football, any arena where size, maximal aerobic power, and absolute strength determine the winner, but in rock climbing, the importance of many of these factors is minimized by the nature of the sport.

While women fall short in absolute strength compared to men, with training they can develop a high strength to weight ratio. The strength needed by the climber is determined largely by physical stature. Lynn Hill, for example, weighs 105 pounds, probably twenty to forty pounds less than even the trimmest of her male counterparts. Women do have a higher proportion of body fat, but this is a characteristic which varies greatly on an individual basis. In a series of experiments conducted in the laboratory, J. Wilmore, a board member of the American College of Sports Medicine, concluded that for the three major components of athletics, strength, endurance, and body composition (lean/fat ratio), the differences between the best female and male athletes are few. However, because many women do not begin any kind of athletic training program until much later than the average male, relative strength gains are often greater in females than males, following similar weight resistance training programs.

In general, women are considered to have better balance and flexibility than men when they start climbing. This tendency, coupled with a shortage of strength, often helps women to develop better style and technique in their early climbing experiences. Since use of the feet is critical to compensate for a lack of power, the woman who becomes seriously involved in climbing often has superior technique to complement the strength she gains through climbing and training. Men often face a different task, and must learn how to conserve strength, rather than rely on it.

In reality, the physical limitations on women rock climbers seem to be relatively insignificant. Every handicap seems to have an advantageous counterpart. Given the lack of absolutes in the game, women need only capitalize on their strong points and work on their weak ones to hold their own with the best. Undoubtedly women would be at a disadvantage were climbing ever to become a competitive sport in categories like "World Fist Crack Champion." By the same token, females might well set the standard on slabs and thin cracks. Climbing is climbing, and the major components of the sport remain the same, regardless of the gender of the climber. As we all know, the rock really doesn't care. What matters is that particular blend of qualities the individual brings to the sport. The talents that distinguish the best are both physcial and mental. Any seasoned climber recognizes the role positive thinking plays in extending personal limits. For many of us it is the primary source of our addiction. When I am climbing at my best, the only voice getting air time in my internal dialogue is clear and confident--I am convincing myself of my ability to succeed. That other pest, The Confidence Eroder, scourge of my ambitions, ("It's a long reach, you'll take a forty-footer...") is held in check, mute. Unfettered by doubt or fear, my body is free to interpret a climb with grace and finesse.

Rosie Andrews is one of America's leading women rock climbers and has worked in the outdoor field in a number of capacities. She has worked as an instructor for Outward Bound Leadership School, Outdoor Program specialist at the University of Vermont, and as a manager of Rock and Snow, a climbing shop in New Paltz, New York. She was one of the owners and a director of Sheer Adventure, a rock climbing guide and lecture service. She currently works for a specialized climbing apparel manufacturer.

Rock Climbing: The Lasting Love Affair
Beth Bennett

To understand the deep and long-lasting effect that climbing has had on me, my childhood history is of paramount importance. When other girls were reading Nancy Drew and the Bobsy Twins I was devouring Tarzan novels. I always envisioned myself as the hero (never the heroine), swinging from boughs, rescuing the underdog, and living as a Rousseau-an enfant savage. Although I don't believe that this literary menu led to my involvement with rock climbing per se, I do think that my early identification with the active role contributed to the approach I later took toward climbing.

When I had grown up somewhat (at least beyond the point where I was reading Tarzan by flashlight under the covers) I did attempt to undertake a more typical feminine activity: modern dance. While I never would have been invited to join the Martha Graham group (or even the local performing arts group), several years of plie and relevee and reckless jete did instill in me an appreciation of balance and grace and artistic technique. Whether or not I ever attained a mastery of any of these attributes as a dancer is another question. It was much easier for me to develop a sense of balance on a vertical face than on the dance floor, and I believe the grace of a good climber executing a difficult sequence rivals that of a world class ballerina. Having seen many 5.8 climbers who can leave me in the dust on the pull up bar, I am convinced of the value of good climbing technique. It took me years before I got past the one pullup stage--which didn't stop me from leading 5.10 (although I was worthless on even easy over-hangs until I developed some upper body strength).

When an aspiring boyfriend took me climbing for the first time these isolated events of my past were catalyzed and I fell in love with rock climbing, the longest lasting love affair of my life. Despite the fact that it's been over 15 years since that first 5.5 slab in the Linville Gorge area in North Carolina, vignettes of those (and many other) climbs still remain clear and vivid. Perhaps more than any other aspect of climbing, this is my most treasured, that I can recall with startling clarity favorite, isolated sequences from past climbs, as if I were picturing the face of a good friend. This playback procedure is probably similar to the process of visualization, encouraged by coaches of many sports in order to place athletes mentally in situations with which they will have to contend during competitive events. In my case, this re-enactment may not be as effective as a strict visualization, but on the other hand, I don't do it to improve my climbing, but rather because I enjoy the memory. I see that little edge, and the toe of my boot centered on it, rocking my knee over my foot and standing up. It's a little like seeing a favorite movie over and over, in that the suspense, the not-knowing is not there. I know I am not going to fall, that my foot does stay on that hold, there is a hidden handhold around the corner, that tenuous jam doesn't slip when I move the other hand up. One part of me enjoys the suspense while I'm climbing, but another, more bucolic part of my mind likes the rerun better.

So what are these vignettes like and what do I get out of them? Perhaps the best answer is to give a few illustrations.

Years later, I still tense up and get nervous when I think back to my first forty footer (fall). I had reached the top of a bulge on a 5.9+ route on the Bastille in Eldorado Springs called Blind Faith. Most people jam the crack through the bulge. At that point, I hadn't been exposed to many cracks, and I hadn't figured out how to jam. So I climbed the face. At that time, I was opposed to chalk, especially in Eldorado where the white blotches permanently marred the red rock. (I have since seen the error of my ways!) I can never forget the feeling of inevitability and awful resignation as my hands slimmed slowly off the rounded holds at the top of the bulge. In the days immediately following this debacle, I returned mentally to that bulge too often for comfort. Yet, I think this process of recall is beneficial in that it allows one to explore alternatives: Why didn't I lunge for the bucket?! Why didn't I climb the crack? Why didn't I put in another nut? These alternate scenarios might be more readily applied next time, and thus this process can afford a real learning experience.

The Naked Edge is arguably one of the most beautiful climbs anywhere, because of the quality of the climbing and the position, high on the Red Garden Wall overlooking all of Eldorado Canyon and the South Boulder Creek drainage. I'd wanted to climb the first pitch ever since I saw it: a steep finger crack in a shallow dihedral, which blanks out near the top of the pitch. I've done the route too many times to count now (having participated in a filmed documentary with Lynn Hill in 1980 added at least 10 repeats to the grand total). My first foray (still without chalk) was memorable simply because my forearms were so exhausted ('pumped') that each move near the top of the pitch was fairly dynamic--when I reached the buckets I was still afraid I couldn't hold on.

Then there was the day boldering on Flagstaff when I fell on my butt after sliming off the chalked and greasy holds of an easy problem. Now, chalk is funny stuff--one uses it to cut down on sweaty hands and fingers and augment the cohesiveness of hand to rock but when rock is overchalked, it becomes extremely slick, and virtually necessitates the use of chalk to overcome the lack of friction developed by the magnesium carbonate overlay. I had never believed this until that day on Flagstaff. Frustrated and humiliated by landing on my rear end in the dust in front of a crowd, I grabbed a chalkbag and proceeded to walk up a half a dozen boulder problems I had never succeeded at before. I've been an avid chalker ever since. (Although I must add, parenthetically, that I still disapprove of over-chalking--rubbing the chalk well into one's hands not only decreases the overload on the rock, but also results in a better friction.)

One really rewarding aspect of climbing is the potential for developing close friendships with a partner. One of my earliest partners is still a dear friend: Pat Adams. Together we did the third free ascent of the Yellow Wall on the Diamond, Long's Peak. The memories of many pitches of long, clean hand cracks run into one another, but the joy and closeness we felt when we topped out, just moments before the afternoon thunderstorm began are crystal clear. As is the memory of the long walk out and cramming into a small Peugeot with three other climbers from New York and all their gear who took mercy on us as we hitched back to Boulder. On many other occasions Pat and I used the old ploy of 'boy hide in bushes, girl stick out thumb'. The potency of these memories of friendship is only enhanced by the beauty of the experiences that were shared.

Another experience with Pat is still vivid in my memory but because I at least was absolutely terrified and physically miserable. We were trying to free climb the Diagonal Direct, a long line on the lower East Face of Long's Peak, leading up to the Diamond. A combination of free routes up the lower face and on the Diamond itself gave the possibility of a Grade VI, an exciting idea as it had not been done at that time. The first several pitches went well despite Pat's disdain for my use of a cheater rock to begin the first move (as the snow had melted more than usual that year, I couldn't reach the first holds!). We rapidly reached the point at which the regular Diagonal route rappels into a second corner system and began to climb past. Unfortunately for our dreams of glory, the runoff from above left the leaning crack system of the Diagonal Direct full of mud and running water. After several falls, we decided to rappel into the regular route, but the afternoon thundershower decided to gainsay us by appearing in midmorning after we had rappeled--an action which cannot be undone once the ropes were pulled. The climb back up the repel was frighteningly unprotected and involved using crack-n-ups (small, anchor shaped devices ranging from 1/8" to 1/4" in width) as points of aid. The sleet and howling wind added considerably to my tension and misery. The rappel down the diagonal crack system was a fitting culmination to an extremely unpleasant day as we careened across the wall, slipping on wet rock trying to make the necessary pendulums to reach the belays. Nonetheless, we could laugh and joke at ourselves and our plight--an important element of a good climbing partnership.

During an experiment with biofeedback I was asked to focus on an experience which I found relaxing, and then on another which I felt to be unpleasant. For a pleasant experience, I recalled a fine day's climb: the fall weather was lovely, the breeze pleasant, the sky clear and blue, the rock warm and friendly. Oddly, this memory generated more stress as perceived by the machines than did the recollection which I felt to be more stressful. My theory for this discrepancy is twofold. First, as I mentally reenact the moves of the climb, I probably tense the same set of muscles that I use while climbing and muscle tension is picked up by biofeedback machines. Second, climbing is a stressful activity. Apart from the obvious muscular exertion which is a form of stress, there are certain mental stresses associated with climbing engendered by fear of falling, failure, injury, and so on. The combination of mental and physical stresses which I had called up during the biofeedback session were much more apparent to the machines than to me. I think that this is an important point, and perhaps one which accounts for much of the popularity of climbing and other so-called high risk sports. I enjoy and need a certain amount of stress.

From an evolutionary perspective, this apparently harmful proclivity for stress can make sense. In order to stay fit and survive, our ancestors were exposed to high levels of stress incurred in a hunting and gathering lifestyle. I think it's very likely that humans evolved with high stress levels as a typical part of their environment and consequently still have the tendency to function best under some optimum stress level.

Climbing and other high risk sports are an ideal opportunity to expose oneself to stress, both physical and mental, for a number of reasons. First, the physical exercise of climbing is beneficial (although the tendon and joint injuries which accompany climbing at higher grades are clearly a result of this extreme level and are of dubious physical benefit). At times, climbing may be aerobic, though certainly the hikes to and from all but roadside attractions induce some level of aerobic capacity. The mental benefits from limited exposure to semi-controlled stress situations may be the most important benefit from climbing, although the pleasure derived from the actual experience is arguably the ultimate rationale for pursuing the activity. By routinely exposing oneself to high adrenalin levels, to situations in which one must think fast and act rapidly on the results of those thoughts, and accept the consequences of those actions, one can build up a capacity for dealing with this sort of situation in real life experiences. While situations of such seriousness may be few and far between (e.g. dealing with medical or psychological emergencies) self control and rapid action may be crucial and even life-saving. I would never say that I climb to exercise these mental muscles, but I think their development is a significant by-product of my climbing. But in the end, it's really the wind blowing in my hair, reaching for that little hold and feeling the smoothness of the moves that keep me climbing.

Beth Bennett has been at the forefront of women's climbing for many years and continued to climb at high level while pursuing her Ph.D. in biology and raising her five year old. She has published a number of professional papers in the field of molecular, cellular and developmental biology and she is currently teaching in the department of biology at the University of Colorado, Boulder.

Arlene Blum in Annapurna, 1978 were she led the first American mountaineering expedition to reach the summit.

The Tragic Mountain
Arlene Blum

The Aeroflot jet is oppressively crowded, but I feel totally alone. I watch the sun set golden over the Atlantic with a feeling of fatality. I am in a space and time machine and do not know where I will come out. In my purse is a telegram: "Invite you International Alpine Camp Pamir 1974--Sportkomitet USSR." I have only known for a few weeks that I was going to Russia to climb Peak Lenin, a mountain over 23,000 feet high.

Before I left New York, I called home for messages. There was a letter from Fay Kerr, a New Zealand friend. Her women's expedition to the Indian Himalayas was hit by an avalanche. Four climbers were killed. Again friends were killed in the mountains. I feel completely resigned, an automaton being propelled to an unknow fate.

Why am I flying to Moscow alone? Climbers usually go on expeditions together. I won't meet my climbing companions, Heidi Ludi, Eva Isenschmidt, and Margaret Munkle, until I get to Russia. They are Swiss women from RENDEZ-VOUS HAUTE MONTAGNE, an international women's climbing club to which I belong. I have Heidi's warm letters urging me to join them in the Pamirs, but still, I know nothing of their personalities, ambitions or even their climbing ability.

The Russians have invited 180 climbers from ten western countries to climb in the Pamirs, a range of high, rugged mountains near the Chinese border. Since it's the first time American climbers have been allowed to visit the Pamirs, there has been a great deal of excitement about it in the States. A dozen experienced women expeditionary climbers applied to be part of the American team. We were all turned down, which is why I'm going with the Swiss. Two strong women climbers without previous expedition experience were invited. The men climbers were selected from those who had applied and had previous expeditionary experience. I discussed this with a woman climbing friend who had also applied and been turned down.

"I heard a rumor that when the Americans chose their team," she said sweetly, "they wanted to make certain that any women along would be ladies."

A TYPICAL DAY AT LENIN BASE CAMP

The breakfast gong sounds. I yawn and stretch luxuriously on my thick foam mattress. Then I put on my tennis shoes and stroll out between row upon row of identical tents.

The Russians are staging this "sportscamp" to raise hard currency for a Himalayan expedition next year. They're charging us $750 each, and trying hard to give us our money's worth. There are hot showers, volleyball and soccer fields and movies at night. The accommodations are surprisingly--even amusingly--lavish. Everything lives up to the glossy full-color brochure with the invitation, "Well-known Soviet climber Vitaly Abalakov wishes you to conquer the Pamirs."

The Russians have put flagpoles with our national flags in front of the tents, so the camp has the air of a people's summit meeting. I smile as I pass the British tents. Abalakov and the other Russian "Masters of Sport" have been a bit scandalized by the casualness of the British climbers, especially their way of naming a new leader every day. Two nights ago in the middle of the night the British took down their own flag and raised a pair of lace panties. But when they straggled out at dawn, grinning broadly and ready to salute, another British flag was waving proudly.

In the mess tent, the tables are laden with smoked salmon, hot sweet Russian tea and beluga caviar. I smear a thick slice of dark Russian bread with sweet butter and then pile it high with caviar. Extravagant, but it seems to be plentiful here. (Later, when I priced caviar in Moscow, I found I'd been eating $30 worth every morning.)

I look for a place to sit and eat. In fact, finding a chair in the crowded mess tent is one of the few serious practical problems of the day. The Austrians and the Germans, who are assigned to the first sitting, like to linger on, so there's never quite enough room for the rest of us. The tent is jammed with climbers chatting in a complex mixture of languages. There are the three elderly Italians--one in his 70s. I don't see the French; they must be making an even better breakfast from the cases of pate, chestnut paste and pop-top cans of wine they brought along. Heidi and Eva are at a German-speaking table. I feel too sleepy for a German lesson. The Americans are here, but I'm shy of sitting with them since I wasn't invited to join the team.

I decide to sit with a group of English-speaking Russians. Elvira Schataeva, the leader of a group of nine Russian women, is talking animatedly about the problems of organizing an all-woman expedition. "Most Russian men just didn't think an all-woman party could climb a 7,000-meter peak," she says. Lenin has not yet been climbed by a group of women and either Elvira's party or ours my be the first. "What route do you plan to take?" I ask. "We plan to traverse the entire summit of Lenin climbing the East Ridge and descending the Razdelny route."

"We were planning to go up by the Razdelny route, but why don't we go together?"

"This is impossible." She doesn't say why, but I sense that the Russians want their women to make the first all-woman ascent without us.

She smiles. "We cannot climb together, but we can celebrate together. We'll have a great party after the climb." She is so confident of success. As we wander out of the mess tent toward the Russian encampment, she says, "Our group is very strong. We have strong collective spirits and will stay together no matter what happens." I wonder a bit as I look at the inadequate Russian equipment--the heavy cotton tents with button closures, the flimsy wooden tent poles, the clumsy, old-fashioned nailed boots. The light from the icy summit of Peak Lenin shines on Elvira's golden hair.

Today we're to begin carrying loads to Camp I. I'm eager to get started, but Heidi and Eva want to bathe first. The Swiss have brought an inflatable orange-and-yellow bathtub, and they spend a surprising amount of time keeping themselves and their clothes clean.

Our plans for the climb must be cleared with our Russian adviser. We stand in a large tent in front of a photomap of Lenin with the routes marked and painfully translate every word from English to German to Russian and back. The discussion seems interminable. He is dubious of the strength of a party of four women, but finally he acquiesces. Then forms with every detail of our daily plans and our expected time of return, must be filled out.

To Western climbers the Russian approach seems rigid and bureaucratic. We're not used to these mass ascents. Everything we want to do here has to be specified in detail and approved. The routes are so well-traveled they seem like highways. There are shortwave radios everywhere, spouting forth messages: "The weather is good. The weather will turn bad. Go up. Go down." Half the time the radios don't work, and weather reports aren't reliable, which confuses things further.

Now that our plans have been cleared, our food and gear have to be organized and packed. An antlike army of climbers has been coming and going between camps on Lenin for several days now, patiently moving supplies up the mountain. At four in the afternoon, our little group finally manages to join their ranks. Big thunderclouds are forming for our daily storms. Our packs are light, so we'll have to make several trips over this terrain. Heidi and Eva and Margaret keep stopping to look at the flowers and chat with climbers coming down the mountain. Things are going so slowly, it seems like we're never going to climb anything. "Stop being an impatient American," I tell myself. I try to join in the conversation, but it's all in German. There's little point in waiting. I carry my load alone.

A NIGHT AT BASE CAMP

Back at base camp that evening, the climbers are sitting around drinking vodka and telling stories. The Russian women come down dancing and singing spirited folk songs. "We've made our second camp in a snow cave," they tell me.

Far into the night I discuss the merits of women's expeditions with some of the men. Half the groups here are all men. The British, who have no women among them, say flatly, "Most women climbers aren't first-rate. They're not really serious. They're so eager to succeed and prove their ability that they don't exercise good judgment."

"But attitudes like that are exactly what make it so difficult for women to GAIN experience and judgment."

"Besides, women can never get along with each other."

"That's ridiculous. I climbed McKinley with five other women. We got along well and made the climb without serious problems. There have even been physiological studies that show that women adapt to altitude more readily than men." They shake their heads and smile paternally.

Bruce Carson and Fred Stanley come bursting in. "We were caught in an avalanche below Krylenko Pass. We think seven people have been buried."

"Do not worry," the Russians say, "Abalakov, a Grand Master of Sport, is confident that no one has been killed."

Still we continue to worry, until some Japanese climbers come down with news that no one has died. Weary, I go back to my tent, turn off the electric light and crawl into my sleeping bag.

THE SUMMIT DAY ON PEAK LENIN

A glorious morning. Nine climbers from Switzerland, Germany, Japan and the U.S. are preparing to leave Camp III at 20,000 feet for the summit. Margaret, who is in her 50s, isn't feeling well and has stayed behind, so Heidi and Eva and I are going on alone. But the Russian advisers tell us, "A storm is coming in. You shouldn't try for the top today."

I wonder if they're saying that because the Russian women have not reached the summit yet either. They must be climbing from the other side along the East Ridge today.

I'm worried about Eva. She has been feeling ill for several days. I've been trying to persuade her to eat and drink more, but neither of the Swiss seems convinced when I tell them dehydration causes altitude sickness. Yesterday they just lay in the tent all day. When I tried to get them to drink, they said, "Leave us alone."

They want to carry just enough gear for an emergency camp. I feel an emergency camp on the exposed summit ridge will be too dangerous. "Let's go light and try to get up and down quickly," I suggest. "If we run out of time we'll have to turn back without reaching the top."

We can't reach a consensus, so I decide to try for the top by myself, going light, with the intent of turning back at two in the afternoon. It seems quite safe: The weather is good, the route straightforward, and a trail from the footsteps of other climbers leads to the summit. Two other people are climbing alone; I can always join them.

I move steadily upward, stopping from time to time to drink some lemonade or eat a candy bar. The going is easy, with spectacular views of the high mountain ranges of Central Asia.

By noontime clouds are forming on the neighboring peaks, and the wind is rising. I have to fight my way against the gusts to the top of a steep section on the ridge. As I move along the level, it begins to snow heavily. I continue upward.

The storm is becoming more violent. Damn it. I have to go down. The summit can't be far above, but to go on alone would be stupid.

The storm has obliterated the tracks behind me, and the whiteout obscures everything. I go down a few hundred feet. The terrain doesn't look right. I retrace my steps hurriedly before they are blown away. I try again to find the right way down. And again. "You may really have blown it this time kid. Your're really alone up here at 23,000 feet."

After a few minutes it clears up a bit. I see the way down. I start down, moving as fast as I can. Ahead of me I can see another figure fighting the storm, coming upward toward me. It's a Swiss climber. "Geben Sie mir Wasser." he gasps. "Oh, good," I think, as I give him my water, "someone to go down with." He drinks and then abruptly leaves, heading upward.

Another apparition in the storm--this time running down behind me. It's Jed Williamson, an American. "Did you get to the top?" I ask him. "No." We descend together in silence.

Farther down at about 3:00 we find Heidi, Eva and Anya, a German climber, huddled in the snow with the storm raging about them. "We are bivouacking here," Eva says. "Stay with us. We can surely reach the summit tomorrow."

In my faltering German, I say, "I am through with Peak Lenin. I am going down. Come with me, it is too dangerous to stay here without tents or stoves."

"No. We will be safe here. Stay." I try to convince them to leave, but my struggle alone in the storm has left me too tired to argue anything with anybody, especially in German.

I stumble down behind Jed. The wind blows me off my feet. I sit there. Finally I get up. Are we really going the right way?

The snow is up to my thighs and the wind is driving crystals of ice into my face. I am so tired. We seem to have been fighting our way down for an eternity.

We stumble into a break in the ridge. It's the break that leads to high camp. As we step down into the sheltered camp, there's sudden silence and relief from the storm.

I collapse outside the tent too tired to take off my crampons. A Dutch climber, Hans Bruyntjes, helps me. I crawl into my tent but can't sleep. Of the nine climbers who left our camp this morning, only Jed and I have returned. The other seven are somewhere above us on the summit ridge, exposed to the full fury of the storm without tents, stoves or sleeping bags. I pray that they are all right.

AGAIN, CAMP I ON PEAK LENIN

After the severity of the last few days, the rock and ice down here seem warm and soft. A stream of climbers files by on their way back to the luxuries of base camp. Among them are Molly Higgins and Marty Hoey, the two women on the American team, who both climbed strongly and reached the summit before the storm broke.

Somehow, I do not want to go down with the others to base camp, to leave the mountain for the last time. Things up here are still unresolved for me. Only six climbers came down to camp the morning after our summit attempt. Eva died of exposure in the storm that night on the exposed summit ridge. So senseless. If only I had tried harder to persuade her to come down with me. If only things had been different.

Why, oh, why could the weather not have been like this a couple of days ago? Today when no one is climbing, when it doesn't matter, it is perfectly still and beautiful. If only things had been different.

I keep seeing Eva bending over the flowers. She was such a slight person. She really didn't seem to belong on a harsh mountain. It didn't have to happen. But then I think, "Who are you to say where she belonged?"

I sit here piling rocks into unstable configurations, unable to summon energy to do anything more complicated than see if I can add one more rock to the tower without causing it to collapse.

Three Americans--Allen Steck, Christopher Wren and Jock Glidden--come down from a different side of the mountain. They say they reached the top of Lenin yesterday. As the storm raged they had been camped high on the summit ridge. "Our tent pole broke in the storm. We kept our clothes and boots on continuously for several days in case the tent was destroyed.

"When the storm finally ended, we started for the summit. Someone was lying in the snow. It was a body--Elvira Shataeva. We went farther and found another body, then the remnants of a tent and two more bodies."

The Americans think that some of the women were too weak to go farther and the others stayed with them instead of going for help. Their equipment was poor. Their stoves probably failed so they couldn't melt snow for water to drink or eat. Their cotton tents were blown apart as they huddled there for warmth. We hear that the women radioed the base camp that one woman had died and two others were sick. Then, on the third day of the storm, Elvira and another Russian must have decided to go down--too late.

People are sitting around speculating about why the Russians didn't radio the other climbers on the mountains to form a rescue party. There has been no official announcement at all, but we have heard that Elvira radioed, "Goodbye, we are going to die."

I can't think of anything but the irony of today's warm sunny weather. If only it had come a few days earlier. Everything would have been completely different. Right now we might all be down in base camp celebrating.

My rock tower crumbles. I think of this summer in the Pamirs. About 200 climbers attempted to reach the top of Peak Lenin; 100 succeeded, 13 died.

The sun shines. The top of Lenin seems so close above me I can touch it.

ARLENE BLUM is a well-known mountaineer, lecturer, biochemist, and author. She has taken part in climbs of Mt. Everest and Mt. McKinley, and led the first American ascent of Annapurna I.

Arlene is currently completing a history of women in mountaineering, is on the Board of Directors of Earth Island Institute, and presents motivational lectures and workshops on leadership.

A Mountain Experience
Julie Brugger

When my parents asked me where I wanted to go to college, I said "Somewhere with mountains." I thought I really wanted to go to MIT and be a mathematician but I knew that, although I may have been one of the smartest kids in my high school, I had been too much of a nonconformist and troublemaker and I could never get the requisite recommendations from my teachers. I suppose they would shake their heads now and with knowing looks say "We knew she would come to no good" and with a secret smile I would do nothing to undeceive them.

Why mountains? I had never lived anywhere there were mountains, hardly had seen any, and certainly had never climbed one. But mountains are the ultimate symbol of man's striving, and even then I must have known how strongly the struggle was to pervade and shape my own life.

I had always been the shy and quiet type and assumed the role of not-so-impartial observer, wondering at the antics of my fellow creatures. I could find no meaning in their endless preoccupation with their appearance and the impression they made, and the cruel games they played with each other. I could never be sure whether it was them or me who was crazy. Of one thing I was sure, I did not belong, and I wondered if there was a place in this world that I would ever feel I did.

So I came out to Washington to go to college, away from the Midwest whose horizons were as empty as what life there seemed to offer. The University was large; I could remain anonymous and undisturbed while I searched for my own path. In this mode of detached curiosity, one day I wandered into a Climbing Club meeting and watched beautiful slides of rugged black mountains pushing their way above the lush green forest and valley, above the corrugated white glaciers, and sprawling across the horizon under a sky of such an intense blue as I had never known existed. There was so much space, so much possibility. The mountains seized my imagination and I felt that I already knew more about them than I possibly could have, felt that hidden beyond some shadowy ridge or sparkling on some distant sun-touched summit maybe some kind of answer awaited me.

I wanted to go out into those mountains at once and signed up for a beginner outing for the very next weekend. I quickly learned that the mountains do not offer their possibilities to the unskilled and unknowledgeable. Their ways must be learned--their weather, how to travel, how to be safe, how to overcome fear, how to respect. In order to do that I found a summer job in the city instead of returning home so that I could take the Basic Climbing Course from the University on the weekends. I never went back to the Midwest again except to visit.

That summer I learned how to tie knots and how to handle the ropes to belay my partner and travel safely on glaciers. I learned how to read maps and use a compass to navigate in unknown or obscured terrain. I learned how to employ the mountaineer's intimidating ice axe and crampons to ascend an icy slope or arrest a dangerous fall. I learned that with the right equipment and clothing it is possible to be safe and relatively comfortable in diverse weather conditions. I learned how to find the weaknesses in a sheer rock wall and use them to climb it. My excitement grew and with it my desire to learn more. With every small summit came a triumph out of proportion to its size. It came from a growing certainty that I had found my path and set my boot upon it, all of the signs pointed that way.

There was the beauty of the physical environment. Cool, shady forests with trees so straight, tall, silent and covered with moss that they gave me the impression of being as old and as wise as the earth. Wildflowers that exuberantly crowded the meadows, stood proudly alone, or hid shyly away, and each urged me to learn its name. Crystal clear water that tumbled noisily down rocky streambeds, or tapped a quiet rhythm as it melted from a protected pocket of the last winter's snow, and always invited me to drink. Snow in all of its forms, from the soft white blanket that quiets and blurs the winter landscape to the hard, metamorphosed, twisted forms that reared up or plunged down vertically all around me in the glaciers. Rocks of every hue and description. Rocks that were so solid they could support my weight on a sliver as thin as a dime and rocks that crumbled beneath my touch, and all gave off that distinctive odor of ozone when struck one against another. Mountains of all temperaments, some calm and majestic, some playful, some truculent, and some downright malevolent, and each offering me its own promise of adventure and challenge and reward.

And above all that, the piercing blue sky. It was a place big enough for me to breathe and not feel a constriction in my chest, a place where my heart could expand and never get too big to fit. The wildness of it spoke to the wildness in me.

And there was the delight in getting to know this body that I am living in. I had never been good at any athletic activities and I considered myself uncoordinated and inept, but my desire to be in the mountains made my determination strong and I discovered that with time, patience and practice, I could learn most anything, some people just learn faster. Then, when I have learned, there is the pure joy of the movement, hiking steadily for hours with a heavy pack, or executing a series of delicate maneuvers on the rock, or skidding dizzily down a steep snow slope at breakneck speed but in complete control. I am in tune with my body, fit, and free. The feel of my heart pounding in my chest, the smell and sting of my sweat, the strong, smooth flexion and expansion of my muscles and their satisfying and relaxing ache at the day's end, all let me feel and rejoice in my aliveness. I can communicate with this human machine. I know when to listen to its murmurs and aches and pains and when to ignore them and exert my will and push it to its limits. I can respect those limits but I know how to expand them as well.

And there were the many challenges to face and the opportunity that each one offered for me to grow. The challenge of trying something I don't know if I can do and giving it the very best I have to give, to chart my depths by plumbing them. The challenge of admitting my fear, facing it, and overcoming it, and in overcoming it finding I can stop avoiding having to face it again. The challenge of accepting failure as a possibility, inevitable sometime, and not due to personal deficiency, a chance to learn more about myself and what I can do differently the next time. The challenge of summoning total concentration for a difficult move, of tuning out the world and harnessing every muscle, every nerve, every brain cell, every heartbeat for the task at hand, to transcend, literally, to climb over.

For the first time in my life I found people I could relate to. My coursemates were a varied lot, young and old, students, couples, scientists, carpenters. Yet we all shared this developing love for the mountains. Sitting around the campfire at night, their faces shining with firelight and the excitement of the day, their smiles and laughter felt real to me. Simple conversations became a pleasure instead of an inanity. Shared adversity built trust and stripped away pretensions and the other excess baggage people carry around to deal with their complicated world. These things have no use in the mountains. Apparent now, for me to see, was their sincerity, their enthusiasm, their sense of humor, their scrappiness, and I realized that, among people such as these, I could feel some sense of belonging.

But most of all there was the great laughter building inside of me, an urge to throw back my head and stretch out my arms and shout my happiness to the world.

At the end of the course two of the other students and I decided to climb Mt. Rainier although our instructor told us he did not think that Basic students were ready for such a climb. We went anyway and you never saw three more scared, sick, sunburned, tired, and exhilarated people as drug themselves down from the summit that day. It was our first climb all on our own and although now I know how easy it was, scarcely another has given me such satisfaction. By the end of the summer I was little different on the outside, maybe a bit more tan in the face, more definition in the muscles, more ready with a smile, but on the inside a small, slow flame had begun to burn and spread its warmth outward, an orphan child had discovered she had a home.

In the fall I took a Rock Climbing course and the flame leaped and crackled as I learned new techniques and expanded my skills and watched the colors change and felt the nights get colder and my friends gather closer around the campfire. When the course finished I continued to find other novice climbers and together we would attempt routes of increasing difficulty, sometimes scaring ourselves to death, sometimes failing miserably, and sometimes succeeding with remarkable ease, but always learning and increasing our confidence in our ability.

My first boyfriend was a climber and when school was over we took up the lives of "climbing bums," much to my parents' dismay, and journeyed all over the West to different climbing areas in a beat-up red Volkswagen, living on granola and peanut butter sandwiches and wearing baggy green Army pants and heavy leather boots, the climber's uniform of the day. We went to California and Canada, Washington and Wyoming, and everywhere could be found that unearthly blue sky. I learned to love the freedom of that life. It was life reduced to the bare essentials--no bills to pay, no schedules to meet, no decisions to make except what to have for dinner and what to climb the next day. I learned a sense of self-reliance from bivouacking in snow storms with no food and minimal equipment, from do-it-yourself Volkswagen repairs on the road and making the money that most people spend in a weekend last the whole summer, to deciding which risks to take in the mountains and which to forego. In the company of one so highly skilled I quickly expanded my definition of the possible--how far it was possible to hike in a day, how much it was possible to carry, how hard of a rock climbing move it was possible for me to do--and learned that the limits of possibility are often self-defined. My joy at being in the mountains did not diminish, it only grew. The future that middle class American society offered held no attraction for me. The things that I found were important--health, freedom, love, and the continuation of the struggle--could not be had for money. It became clear to me that I could never live a normal life, that there was too much living to be done than could fit into weekends and two weeks vacation a year.

But more enlightening than all of these, I learned how to love someone and what it means to have a real friend. Always I had been so painfully aware of my separateness, I felt a yawning gap between my feelings and perceptions and those of other people, and now I became aware that it was possible to touch another person and be touched and momentarily bridge that gap. By sharing my love of the mountains I gained the courage to share other parts of me as well, and found that they could be accepted, and understood, and even loved. I learned the quiet happiness of sharing the rituals of everyday life, of getting to know someone's ways, of the superfluity of words.

So we stretched our money as far as it would go, and when it gave out we did whatever we could to make a little more, just enough to go on another climbing trip. For two years we lived this life of vagabonds, my dedication and enthusiasm never flagged, I felt I could live like that forever.

The mountains took my first love. It was in the fall and he was working on the apple harvest. I was on a rock climbing trip to Yosemite where he soon would join me. I had been working a 9 to 5 job for six months in the city and was impatient for the outdoors. He had gone out climbing on a day off, there was a rockfall, my friend was suddenly and incomprehensibly and forever gone.

I knew where to run. I went to the city, stood numbly through the funeral, loaded up the old Volkswagen, mine now, and went to the mountains. The pain and the loss were so great, but climbing could take all my energy and concentration and let me forget for awhile. I cried on all the belay ledges. With tears streaming down my face I sang all the songs that reminded me of him and our life together, sang to the trees and streams and rocks and glaciers and summits while the sun poured down from the constant blue sky. There, in those places where we had shared so much, I was reminded too often of him. I was alone again and feared that I would always be alone. But the mountains were still there all around me, my love for the mountains was still there, it would always be there, could never be lost. It gave me the strength and courage to continue on the path I had chosen, knowing that there would always be beauty and joy in life. I became perhaps quieter and more reticent again, and although those around me thought I took it so well, I was dying inside. But I pushed on. California to Canada, Washington to Wyoming, always there was a challenge to be met, another mountain beyond the one just climbed, the sapphire sky, and the emptiness to be filled.

I did some of my best climbing then. I was on my own, the responsibility was all mine. I had no one of greater skill or experience to rely on. The only other thing that had been important to me was gone, so I had all of my energy for myself. And I had a manic amount of energy. I led my first 5.10 then and, I suppose, broke an important barrier for myself, though it didn't seem very significant to me at the time, since only part of me was there. I had never even dreamed of doing it; it was something that the best climbers I knew still spoke of with awe. But my partner and I had done all the 5.9's we could find in Yosemite, and all there was left was something harder. I tackled more difficult mountain climbs as well, and climbed some of the forbidding north faces in the Canadian Rockies. Eventually, days could go by when I didn't cry, and slowly, slowly, the pain went away.

The mountains brought my second love. I had seen him around for years, wearing the look that says stay away, and now I felt drawn toward him. I had looked out of those same eyes and knew the feelings they could be hiding. I felt a kindred spirit behind the walls, one to share my love of life and mountains with and it was time to share again. I had learned to lose and live and I was no more afraid of those adamantine walls than I was of those of granite on which we danced our intricate dance. I was used to challenges and I was not afraid of hard work. It was both of these. But, in time, like our mountain ranges, the peaks and valleys rolled out behind us and one day we could look back and see how far we'd come.

We grew even closer than I could have imagined. We shared so many of the same thoughts and feelings. Our sense of our differentness from the world and our similarity to each other strengthened the bond. Our love for the wild places and a need to continually seek challenges took us from climbing to skiing and kayaking and bicycling the backroads and running the trails.

Anything to be in the mountains! Skiing in the winter--good, hard work climbing up and a chance to concentrate and improve my technique on the way down, or on a day when everything comes together, to really fly. Winter can be a friendly season for those who have the right equipment and can keep moving to keep warm, and there are many rewards it has to offer. My favorite days are when the sun is out and it's so cold the moisture in the air crystallizes and sparkles all around you like visible magic. I think the only thing that keeps me sane working through the rainy Northwest winter is knowing that all that rain is making big piles of snow for me to play in on the weekend, that a big gulp of fresh air and realness will help get me through another week.

Kayaking takes me to mountains that climbers would scarcely look at, too tame, but they have something to offer those who look other places than just upward. Water. Rivers each have their own color and personality and snowfed streams have the same magic sparkle as a cold winter day. In the winter I slide down it on my skis, in the summer in a boat, but it's the same leaping, laughing water spirit bearing me along.

Bicycling on the twisting mountain roads, the swiftness of my passage gives me a different perspective on the mountain environment and the flowing rhythm of the movement frees my mind to wander as it will and explore new possibilities.

When the now ubiquitous running shoe first appeared, climbers were quick to discard their clunky old boots and take to the trails in those wings of nylon. Hiking in the summer in shorts and running shoes with only a fanny pack, feeling the miles fly under my feet, watching the mountainscape unroll before me, stopping only for a cookie and a gulp of water, the feeling of lightness and freedom, this must be the closest feeling to heaven (where they are said to wear real wings) on earth.

I found a profession that allowed me plenty of free time to pursue these many activities. I could make good money while I was working, take off on a trip, and then find a new job when I returned. But climbing was still my first love. Because my boyfriend was more of a rock climber than a mountain climber, attracted by the athleticism and extreme difficulty of the moves, I too channeled most of my energy in that direction. I began to train, to lift weights to increase my strength for the most demanding moves. With so much practice, so much time spent on the rock, the tips wore off the ends of my fingers and the rubber wore off the toes of my shoes, and I could climb harder routes than I had ever done before. Yosemite Valley was my home every spring. The smell of the sun on my skin, of bay leaves, of tincture of benzoin that we use to toughen our hands, the formic acid smell of the stinging red ants that abound there, any of these can still evoke the feeling of the sun pouring down from a narrow, blue corridor bounded by walls of rearing granite, heating the rock, raising tiny beads of sweat on my fingertips as I gaze at the tiny seam of a crack splitting a flawless face ("We're going to climb this!?"), or of the life in dusty, crowded Camp IV where climbers' colorful tents jostled against each other like a fistful of jellybeans, but the discomfort went unnoticed at the contented conclusion of a hard day's climbing.

But I missed the mountains, missed travelling with everything I needed on my back, secure in the knowledge that I could go wherever I wanted and handle any situation that arose, missed watching the sun set and rise again, while precariously perched in my tent, high on a ridge, miles from civilization, snug with all I needed to survive. After many seasons pursuing still higher numbers in the rock climbing arena, I wanted to explore new places and try new things. It took little to persuade my friend; he must have been getting more mellow as he got older. We went to Canada in the winter to climb on the frozen waterfalls, to the mountains of South America, the rivers of Idaho, and the canyon country of Utah. There, too, the dazzling blue sky overspread our adventures. It was like the feeling that I had, that in all of these different places, there was always something the same. We were the best of friends and travelling companions. Seeing the excitement in his eyes lifted my heart and fed my own.

It had been all too apparent for years, however, that we could not climb well together. This was a difficult lesson for me. He was too much better than I, too impatient, and not one to hold himself back. He always wanted to lead and I discovered that I could not get as much out of climbing if all I did was follow. It had to be me up there too, me taking the risks, me making the decisions, and me asking for what I needed. And so I had to do things on my own, share my mountains with people who did not mean nearly so much to me as he did, take myself away from the pleasure and security of his company to pursue my own dreams; it was hard for both of us to accept, the distance after so much closeness. But the distance offered a chance for survival of the love that closeness threatened to extinguish.

These are not any astounding revelations, but lessons that people must learn every day. In my case, it seemed that the mountains were always my schoolroom.

We spent many years together, living our lives as we pursued our climbing, always asking for the best from ourselves, never content with less. You might say that we were living in a dream world, avoiding growing up and facing reality. You might say that climbing isolated us from other people and other experiences that would have allowed us to grow in different ways. Still, there could be no price too high to pay for the love and the living and the learning that we shared. The spirit of striving finally led us to question our relationship. It could not work for us in the present as it had in the past and it was time for a change. Certainly we were not afraid of the challenge and the hard work, but could this be a case, as often happens in climbing, when better judgement will lead us to abandon our objective in the face of overwhelming difficulty? Or is it simply that we have gazed too long at the mountain from one perspective and have overlooked an approach on the other side? As I have done before, I know that I will again rely on the lessons I have learned and the strength I have gathered from the mountains to steady me and comfort me as I struggle with the most difficult challenge of my life. I will take my sorrow and my confusion there and be able to find some peace.

The things that brought me to the mountains are the things that keep me there. Their beauty--I never cease to be delighted with sights so simple as a sunrise, tiny flowers greeting me from an unlikely niche they have found high on a windswept peak, a lively lizard scampering across the rock as I struggle for a handhold, a limpid pool reflecting craggy peaks and the cerulean sky. They rouse a voice in me that says "This is why I'm alive." Often, now, the feeling is not that of never-failing astonishment at the beauty of a new prospect, but of welcome recognition and homecoming as I return to the same beloved places time and again.

My body, as I have used and abused it throughout the years, has remained a trusty friend. With good care, I find it can perform, with the benefit of experience, better than it did in its younger days. It is even more important now though, to stay in shape, and I have found city activities--running, swimming, lifting weights, playing soccer, and bicycling--that I enjoy for their own sake as well as for the conditioning I get from them. The feeling of living in a fit and energetic body is so wonderful that, even if I stopped climbing I could not keep a normal working schedule because I wouldn't have time to do all the things I love to do. This old body is always willing to try new things, usually will protest temporarily with sore muscles, but then settles in to its usual slow but steady pace. We have many miles yet to go together.

No matter how far or fast you travel, how many summits you climb, how difficult a move you make, there is always another challenge in climbing--therein lies much of its allure. I am still seeking the challenges--going for something I don't know if I can get, overcoming fear, accepting the possibility of failure, concentrating all my resources on the undertaking--but more and more it seems that the stiffest ones take place, not in the mountains, but in my own life. The lessons I have learned in the mountains are standing me in good stead, but the growth often seems to come, not as it did there, with great joy, but with great pain. Still, each summit reached offers a glimpse of all the others there are to climb.

And still I find friends there aplenty. Some are those I have known for years. Some gray hairs have begun to make their appearance among them. To some I have grown closer throughout the years, and from some I have grown away. But we started climbing together, and though many of them don't climb anymore, we have shared adventures that forged bonds that can never be forgotten. We have belayed, yelled at, laughed with, hugged, competed with, worried about, bivouacked with, pissed off, cried with, and generally well-used each other. What it was that brought them to the mountains, and what it was they got from the mountains they still have within them, and whatever else they do, this we will always have in common. Some are those I have met on my travels, gypsies all, we are bound to meet again. And so we do, in Yosemite or Huaras or Banff or Kathmandu, and share the adventures we've had since last we met. Some are gone forever. They lost their lives in the mountains pursuing their own personal dreams. They live in my memory, forever young, smiling against a backdrop of mountains, the wind ruffling their hair, and come to visit me at odd moments, summoned by an experience that is so like one I had shared with them. And still I find new friends to share my mountains with. I have learned to recognize them by the energy and enthusiasm they radiate, by their shining eyes and animated way of talking. They feel right there, real. They don't have to be climbers, but they usually have a love for the outdoors. These are the people I want to be with, who do what they do out of love. Among these people I can feel like I belong, like we are a small coven of sanity in an otherwise senseless world.

And the great laughter seems to have found permanent lodging in my soul. It bubbles out unexpectedly when I'm going about the business of being a normal person and those around me must wonder at my sudden silliness. It allows me to have a graceful sense of humor about any situation and keeps me from taking anything too seriously. Sometimes it comes on so strong it brings tears to my eyes. It's a little furnace in there, churning out energy that keeps me warm and glowing with life.

At times, feeling a need to accede to the expectations of a society I thought I had rejected, I have tried to use climbing as a means to gain recognition, to be considered a success. I have sometimes got caught up in the pursuit of routes or summits, as a collector pursues butterflies, to capture them, and take the life from them, and display them to the amazement and approval of his colleagues. But these attempts to take the mountains for ambition and not for love have all failed. Because it is not what I have done that ultimately brings me a feeling of peace and belonging, it is doing it. And it is not even what I am doing, but how I am doing it, if it is honestly, joyfully, whole-heartedly then surely I am living as I was meant to live. Climbing, for me, is not a means to an end, nor is it an end in itself. It is a process, and the mountains are the perfect symbol of the process, arid summits, the human spirit in its isolation, mutely and everlastingly reaching for the sky.

If those smug teachers of mine had sent out glowing recommendations to the college of my choice, I could be a math professor now, determinedly writing equations on a dusty blackboard for the enlightenment of students whose faces would be erased and replaced every year. I could have secured my niche in the world and my claim on the American dream. Instead, all of the wealth I own I carry inside me. My security is knowing that what I have, nothing can take away. My ambition is just to get better--at climbing, at understanding, at living. Instead of paying into Social Security for my old age, I pay into a plan that will keep me forever young. Climbing has brought so much into my life and helped to make me the person I am. Even my old diehard father, who for the last fifteen years of my climbing career could only say, "Why don't you go back to school?", has finally recognized this. Upon returning from my first expedition to the Himalayas, a fairly complicated affair requiring fund-raising by selling T-shirts and soliciting donations, in which my father, to my great surprise, heartily participated, I was touched to learn that he had kept a scrapbook of the whole event, which he proudly displayed to me when I went to visit. He was more concerned than I was, I think, about the seriousness of the undertaking and congratulated me on a gallant attempt and a successful return. This from a man who never offered any praise that I can remember when I brought home all those report cards with A's, and for an endeavor that most of society would consider so useless. I am not looking for approval from my parents after all these years, I am just glad that they can recognize how much reward my own path has brought me.

I don't know where my life will lead me, but I know there will always be mountains in it. There is simply a sense of well-being, that all is right with the world, that I get from being there and that I don't want to live without. Someday the challenge will only be to see if I can hobble up a gentle trail to a sweeping vista to gaze at the mountains I used to climb, but I will go to meet it with the same light in my eyes and lift in my heart, knowing that, as sure as that heart-rendingly blue sky will always be found there, so also will be peace and joy.

Julie Brugger was born in Philadelphia. In 1967 Julie settled in Seattle, Washington as a student at the University of Washington and in 1970 graduated with a degree in math and a "terminal passion for the mountains." Since graduation, Julie has made her living as a freelance computer programmer which allows her the freedom to pursue her avocation: climbing mountains.

Cholatse North Face
Catherine Freer

Kathmandu pummels the senses, challenging one to simply cope, after the immediate saturation that follows arrival. And yet the temples seep into consciousness, the beauty of this city strikes a cord wihin us, the dragon image echoes the adventurous spirit that brought us and moves us toward our objective: the unclimbed North Face of Cholatse. (21,130 ft.)

I lounged on the hotel balcony at dusk, absorbing the shock of my return to this dream place. As though on cue, wave after wave of fruit bats left their moorings, heading for their night roosts. They might have been birds except for the peculiar intensity of their whisper flight. Something in the stroke of their wings produced an eeriness, a palpable myster-force.

Pigeon's cooing woke Todd Bibler and me early the next day. We joined Renny Jackson and Sandy Steward, and set about our final preparations amid the rising hubbub in the marketplace. Accommodating our moves to the Nepalese bureaucracy, we juggled our way out of town after only two days. Thirty-seven porters and loads, sirdar, cook, kitchen boy, sahibs, all piled into a truck. The estimated six hour drive to Jiri found us there fourteen hours later. Extricating ourselves from the truck at midnight, we decided the worst was over, and Cholatse would be a breeze.

Next morning bed-tea heralded the beginning of a quieter mood. Life slowed down and came in manageable gulps. There is a rhythm to the days, trekking in. Eating, walking, looking, talking--plenty of time for the land to work its magic on us, for our interior landscapes to respond to the character and subtlety of the exterior landscape. The indigenous people too thrive in this huge, lush, terraced, God's country. They are as determined by the land as by their genes. Transplanted, I fear they would wilt, unsuccored by the vastness, the beauty, the quiet. Soon we all succumb, the view fills our souls, the days obscure the future. We flow through this region coming closer to ourselves.

One afternoon, near the crest of the hill, an old wrinkled woman sat by the side of the trail. I greeted her as we passed. There were crows cawing, circling above. As we turned the next switchback I heard a cawing near her, and I looked back and she was cawing to the crows. She sounded just like them. It seemed that they called back. So there she was, this old woman on a hillside in the afternoon sun and shadow, talking to the birds, living out her life.

The land soothes us when we lay down at night, and resists our penetration by day, putting hills in our way. Yet beckoning. Smoothing off our rough western edges. The valleys open affirmatively towards the peaks. One noon-time we round a corner and there they are, pulling us towards them like a magnet. Unseen 'til now, they'd been pulling all the same. The desire to see our mountain rises to a more prominent place in us. More than before we go to sleep with our dream and it awakens us. We notice each other as partners and recognize the common urgency we feel. This summit is important.

Two weeks, a little less, and we're at base camp, above a glacial blue-green lake, in an idyllic meadow directly across from Cholatse. Taweche, Ama Dablam, and Lobuje rise in the distance. The face is riveting, the weather turning good, and we spend hours a day peering through the telescope, arguing the merits of different lines. It's no easy trick. The couloirs look dangerous, the buttresses slabby and crackless, the "ice runnels" are only plastered spindrift.

We could aid the rock, but gullies go fast. Scouring the face for bivy sites, we wonder if we should take hammocks. I-Tents are lighter. In 6,000 vertical feet there must be a few places to put them. Eventually we agree on a route that zig-zags up the face past a fearsome ice gully toward foreshortened final pitches. We can only speculate from this perspective.

Todd and I turn our attention to the East Ridge of Lobuje, rising dramatically from the town of the same name. A mere three hours approach gains us the familiar feeling--climbing again, looking down on the ravens and lamarghars, the landscape receding suddenly as the days pass with our effort. The climb is good. The jumbled rock is solid or frozen in place. Two pitches speak out: steep face climbing and a smooth dihedral lead me to a belay on the crest. Todd gets a long hand and fist crack up an otherwise blank slab. Two bivy ledges are hard won, and the third night finds us on the summit ridge.

Descending from their ascent of the Southwest Ridge, Sandy and Renny call to us, advising a rope for the summit jaunt. We follow their tracks down the snow shoulders, their curving lines a spectacular frame for the most beautiful views in the world. Back at base camp, we're met with big smiles from growing friendships. Phu Dorje, our superb cook, has baked fruit-nut bread for a celebration tea. We decide unanimously that a good cook is the most essential ingredient in a successful expedition.

The weather was with us on Lobuje. Anxious to take full advantage before a storm, Renny and Sandy leave for Cholatse the next day. We rest another day, reorganizing our food and gear, Todd stalking the summit, always watching. The current finally finds us on the lower slopes, unable to resist the upward directive. All parts of us become subservient to whatever moves us efficiently upward.

The neve that first day was rather good. Base camp hurried away beneath, and soon we were jumaring a rope fixed on a steep rockpitch. Afternoon found the four of us together, pooling our hopes and enthusiasm in anticipation of the climb ahead. Sandy and Renny had fixed three pitches above the bivy. From their highpoint we leapfrogged the lead up toward a vertical bulge of green ice that issued onto a long ramp splitting the upper face.

We avoided the considerable rockfall in the gully, keeping close to the wall, and hoped to be on the ramp above by nightfall. I led a traverse skirting the worst of the rotten snow that characterized these pitches. Renny led past. We neglected to move the belay to a safe corner in our rush to finish the gully and an ice chandelier broke off, crushing my hardhat, giving us a scare and me a terrific headache. Darkness forced us to retreat to sitting bivys.

Next morning, by the time we'd moved back into position to push the route round the corner, the rockfall was already beginning. Todd only had time to do the steepest section before whines too close for comfort forced him back to the belay. We made soup and fiddled away the next four hours, waiting for cooler temperatures to allow us to continue. Just after 2 p.m. Todd finished the pitch with a hanging belay and we were moving again. Renny ran out the next rope and a half, and three more mixed pitches took us to a pretty good ledge, with room for one tent.

By mid-afternoon the following day the character of the route revealed itself definitively. Steep rock, vertical ice, and too much steep, unprotectable, unconsolidated snow. No sunlight meant little thawing and refreezing at that altitude on a north face. We might've known.

Amid all the insecurity, somehow the anchors appeared on cue, a pocket of ice on the verge of despair, or a solid, friendly Friend crack. Before long, ropes were tied off and the troops were moving through, pushing the route until nightfall, sometimes beyond. We had to watch Sandy: the advent of darkness seemed to trigger his adrenalin. One twilight with fierce enthusiasm he threw himself on a vertical rock pitch, viciously hand-jamming against the ice oozing out of the crack. After tenuous aid moves on pins tapped into the ice, he finished the daring pitch and announced happily that he'd found a ledge to bivy on. His enthusiasm called to mind a different scene than reality made available to the rest of us. Renny jumared up and when I saw him lead off again above Sandy, it was as clear as when I saw it myself that the ledge was two foot square. Many hours later we fell exhausted into our tents. In the long night, images of friends and family came larger than memory. My thoughts wove understandings as the spectres danced shadows on the tent walls.

The next days run together, the route finding relentlessly complicated as we moved up the ramp to a horizontal step before the steep ice bowl that led onto the summit ridge. A late-night bivy here seemed cozy until daylight revealed our position. I led off over steep rotten snow with hidden ice runnels. Renny moved through faster than a bear through uphill timber. His pitches always seemed cut from the same cloth--nothing we wouldn't gladly have given away. This time it was a treacherous steep snow pitch; no pro for 165 ft. Sandy tried an alternate path before leading on solid ice up into the steep bowl. Todd ran it out raz-mataz over the intimidating bulge above, and I did the next rope length on good ice and neve. Renny climbed the last pitch in the dark. I was the last to jug home that night with Renny shouting "We're saving you a place." Still gullible, I imagined a big-enough ledge, flatish, ready-made. Well, ready-made it was, a curved porcelain space, too small for the four of us cradled miserably all night.

The moon was still shining close on Makalu's shoulder as bulging mushrooms yielded to the summit ridge early the next day. Seven days of struggle, and we were tired. Dreamlike white towers hung over our heads. The summit looked inaccessible, but over the top was the only way out. We climbed into the mist.

Finally, we were up! What a relief to get what we came for. We paused, surrounded by a dramatic panorama: Everest, Makalu, Cho Oyu, Gyachung Kang.

We didn't want to hurry away but our already rationed supplies made us uncomfortable with the descent still ahead. Two days of rappelling and down climbing the south ridge, a route climbed only once in 1982 by the Swiss, finished our food and fuel and we were met on the moraine by Ongchu Sherpa with tea and chapatis. Radiant smiles all around.

Our plan of lying in base camp savoring the line of the route vanished as afternoon clouds appeared, obscuring the peak, bringing a storm. We hastily decided to beat it down to Thyangboche for Mani Rimdu festival. The instantaneous arrival of the yaks indicated that our sirdar was one step ahead of us, as usual.

We all had different post climb ambitions, but when the time came it was difficult to summon the motivation let alone the necessary energy, and we found our feet trundling down the valleys toward Lukla and airport life.

Catherine Freer began climbing at age 19. At age 37 she was considered by most to be the best woman climber in America. Catherine was killed in 1987 while attempting the second ascent of the Hummingbird Ridge on Canada's Mount Logan. She is responsible for numerous first ascents in many of the major mountain ranges of the world.

Post Card
Sue Giller

March 24,1982

Dear Molly,

We're seven days into the trek now, and my legs have finally recuperated from all the up and down hiking. Somewhere I read that we gain 40,000 feet and lose 30,000 feet in the 120 miles to Namche Bazaar. If I had known that earlier, I'm not sure I would have come.

So far, all goes so well that it's almost scary. We managed to get all of our equipment through Delhi and the Nepali customs with no hassles and a minimum of expense. Once in Kathmandu, we spent a week buying last-minute food, meeting our Sherpa staff, and packing for the trek. The team has been operating superbly--so far all I've had to do is play bara sahib with a few government officials. Tough life! It's good to be back in Nepal again with such a beautiful mountain as our goal. Wish you were here.

April 15, 1982

Dear Molly,

I'm sitting in Base camp, eating dessert (pop corn) and waiting for the evening radio call, to hear how things have gone today up on the mountain. We arrived here (at 16,100 feet) on April 3rd after fifteen days of trekking. The trail follows the same route that traders have used for centuries in trading with Tibet. Indians and Nepalis would travel up to Namche Bazaar (12,000 feet) with lowland items (rice, sugar, spices, cloth) to trade with the highland Tibetans in Namche.

Our trip has been like a journey into the past, as I doubt the lives of the villagers in this region have changed all that much over the past decades and centuries. It is spring here now, and everyone is out in the fields working on the planting. The lowland terraces are being prepared for the rice planting, which will commence with the onset of the monsoon rains in late May. The men and boys are plowing with their water buffalo, while the women are repairing the terraces and their walls. Although some mustard plants and early vegetables are poking through the soil, the land is generally brown and looks barren. I can remember trekking into climb during the late monsoon several years ago. The fields were lush and green, and I felt as though I were inside a giant greenhouse with water and foliage all around. When we came out in October, the rice and wheat had all ripened and the fields were a golden yellow. Now, in contrast, the land seems so dull.

The trail winds up and down, traversing along the edges of fields and going right through the villages. We got a very good look at the life of the inhabitants, and I now appreciate all the more my home in Boulder, with its running water, electricity, and all those things we tend to take for granted in an industrialized society. These Nepalis lead such a rough, physical life, working from dawn to dusk to support a subsistence-level lifestyle, and prey to all sorts of low-grade diseases. The mortality rate for children up to age nine is apparently 50% in some districts, an awesome percentage. Wood is so scarce now after years of over-cutting that it often requires a long day's expedition by the entire family to gather a week's supply of fuel. Many homes are perched on steep hillsides in the middle of the fields, necessitating a one- or two-hour trip for water each day. We saw women grinding wheat by hand. They use large sticks that they bounce up and down in a mortar containing the grain, much like a butter churn with wheat in it. After several hours of this they produce a rough flour used to make chapittis, the flat, unleavened bread tortillas they serve with rice and lentils.

But in spite of this hard life, the people seem to retain a great supply of cheerfulness and friendliness. They sometimes invited us into their homes for tea and potatoes. The porters who carried all of our food and equipment, many of whom are farmers working to pick up a little extra money during slack time in their seasonal work cycle, chattered away with us at the shared rest stops, using limited English and much laughing and gesturing. Even though by their terms we are carrying a fortune in rupees with us, I never feel physically threatened by any of the people I meet here. I think this basic cheerfulness and ease is to a large extent why I've always enjoyed my trips to Nepal so much.

We reached Namche Bazaar, the "chapaty" of the Sherpa people, on March 31. There we traded our lowland porters for hearty, acclimated yaks, and then continued on to base camp. We settled on a sandy beach here, in a small dell formed by several grassy moraines. A small pond provides water and reflects a magnificent view of Ama Dablam and our route. We call the camp Ama Dablam Beach.

We've been working on the mountain for eleven days and seem to be moving along relatively well, although I am getting more and more concerned about the weather. During the first week we had a few showers, but recently we've been getting consistent afternoon snow squalls, and the route has begun accumulating snow. This isn't too bad for the section to Camp I, mostly a long boulder field with little exposure or other hazard beyond a slip with a heavy pack into a hole between two rocks. But the route to Camp II follows a narrow rock ridge and gingerly traverses several steep slabs. They get very slippery, and even with fixed ropes I'm worried about how awkward they might become. A broken leg from a fall on wet rock would necessitate a tricky rescue. Still, I have a great deal of faith in the team members--they were all chosen for their technical capabilities and mountain experience as well as their compatibility.

Another one of my concerns as leader and tactician is the effect the snow is having on the effort to push the route above Camp II. Steep ice slabs predominate there with one rock pitch. I had expected we would take about three days and we still haven't reached the Mushroom Ridge. I originally had Shari, Susan and Stacy fixing lines on this section, but I've asked Lucy and Jini to go up to help with the support, because Shari had said the carries up the rock section were so tiring, and they were all feeling the altitude. Heidi, Anne, and I carried the last load up to Camp II today and came down to base camp to save food higher on the mountain, so laboriously carried up there, and to await word of when Camp III has been established. We will then go back up to Camp II in support of the first summit team.

However, our slowness and these persistent showers potentially create a major problem. We have only so much food for use on the mountain. So if a storm comes in and holds us up for any length of time, or drives us off the mountain for awhile, then I may be forced into a position of having to choose a summit team of only one or two pairs out of the team of eight equal climbers. The rest of us might never get a chance at the summit afterwards. This is a decision I do not want to make. When I accepted Annie's offer to take over the leadership of this trip, I knew I might eventually end up in this position of doling out the prize of the summit to a select few, but I never really understood what such a decision entailed emotionally. How can I make choices among eight healthy, motivated women who have worked for over a year towards one very distinct end? What criteria should I use to pick the lucky two or four who get a chance at the summit?

Indeed, I never really comprehended beforehand how much being the expedition leader would effect my participation in the climb. Certainly on my last two trips to the Himalaya I saw two distinctly different styles of leadership. I was often critical of how certain things were handled, and I thought of how I might handle those situations myself (better, of course). Now that I personally feel the burden of leadership, I begin to see how it changes the perspective of the leader about what is taking place on the trip. I am no longer just "one of the gang" but am an embodiment of some unnamed and unearned "authority," both within the group and to the Sherpas and the Nepalese government. I can no longer act only on my own desires. There is something here much bigger than me.

When talking with Annie on the phone and considering her offer to lead the climb, I thought that my job would largely entail logistics--all those detailed lists of equipment and food, budget projections, and timetables for the movement of people and material on the mountain. Yet I never predicted how all-consuming this attention to logistics would become. I now feel like a mobile computer whose main function is to see that the correct load is at the correct camp in proper time to be used by camps above--i.e., to have the tents for Camp III taken to Camp II soon enough to be moved on when needed, but not taken up too early, thereby displacing another load that would be needed at that camp sooner. Fortunately we only have three camps, so this organizing is relatively easy compared to the six camps on a bigger mountain. Still, I have already redone my charts three or four times. Due to my own perfectionism, I find the mountain has become a logistics ladder that I am trying to have the expedition ascend in as perfect a manner as possible. In this narrowing of horizons, I now realize, I have lost all personal drive to climb the mountain. I no longer care if I reach the summit at all, and this dismays me.

If I had to answer that silly question, "WHY?," I would say that I climb mainly for three reasons. One is for the enjoyment of using my maximal physical and mental abilities to overcome the physiological and psychological problems presented by a climb. Another is for the exciting and magical positions I can reach, such as a small ledge 2000 feet up a granite wall or a snowfield 20,000 feet up a large mountain that drops off thousands of feet around me, knowing that I am at a place few people ever reach, enjoying a view shared only with the mountain gods and that special breed of people who are climbers. Lastly I climb for the camaraderie shared by these fellow climbers, fostered by the shared joys and dread encountered in the intense interdependencies of ropemates. On this trip, however, I seem to have lost touch with all of these rewards, and am instead absorbed by logistics. Because of my self-imposed perceptions of "leadership" and "the role of the leader," I find myself experiencing this trip in a totally different way from any of my other big expeditions.

I am extremely concerned with maintaining the elan of the team--its spirit and unity as a force helping us work together for the summit. As one of the climbers on other trips, I also worried about the sense of unity within the team, but I usually felt it was not my "job" to try to maintain this unity, other than during my own one-on-one interactions with the other climbers. If, for example, there were bad feelings between two climbers, I always felt that it was the responsibility of the leader to straighten out the problem. Well, here I am, the leader, and I begin to see this is no small task. As you know, Molly, I am not the world's most communicative person, but I feel that the answer to resolving intergroup problems lies in open communications. It is the role of the leader to expedite discussions and to help relieve tensions by serving as a channel for the exchange of feelings among people.

The other day, Lucy and I were making a carry from I to II and we ended up traveling together. We talked about a lot of things, including the difficulty of the route, the best way to rig the fixed lines, how everyone was feeling about the food and each other, and what Lucy felt about the climb and the others. Normally, as a team member, I would just voice my own opinions, enjoy the time as a good gossip session, and not really think about the comments other than how they applied to me personally. This time, however, I found myself analyzing every comment, searching for insight into how team members were feeling. I kept wondering: how does this effect the group overall? Should I worry about so-and-so not liking someone else? What can I do about it? Are these comments signs of unhappiness and discontent with the operations of the trip or just normal grousing? How will all of this effect the achievement of the summit, our success as an expedition? Will Lucy take what I say as just a comment from a fellow climber, or will it be The Leader speaking? We were no longer just two friends talking.

In order to make decisions that involve the whole team, I find that I want to know what each climber thinks about the progress of the climb, what her desires and ambitions are in regards to leading and climbing, and who wants to climb (or not) with whom. And I feel that I must subordinate all of my own desires to those of the team, to help maintain group unity and not be accused of misusing my authority. The only way that I have been able to successfully perform this role of group moderator has been to withdraw myself to a reserved position some distance from the team and to try and maintain an overall view of the group and events. This has often caused me to feel somewhat isolated from the team---almost a "them and me" polarization. This is not to say that the others treat me so differently, but that I perceive the world differently because of these self-imposed tasks I feel I must assume to be a "good leader."

Well, enough introspection for one night. As you can see, I'm a little down, but I'm sure things will look better when we finally reach Camp III and I can see some chance of success for the team. Overall I am enjoying the trip immensely and am glad to be on this beautiful mountain with such a compatible group of people.

Dear Molly,

Well, we made it! I can't believe it--we actually got everyone to the top. I always thought it was possible to get all of us up, but I didn't dare expect it--someone usually gets sick or loses her drive for the summit. In fact, it was with this loss in mind that I decided on a team of eight instead of six, even though I thought six was a better number for the trip. I figured if one or two dropped out, then four people would be a little too few for assurity of the summit. But this is a great group and it has shown all along. As these trips go, I can't imagine a smoother one.

Ever since we began gathering the equipment and funds, I've felt the unity and drive of the team. We have been able to stay well within our budget, to avoid losing equipment during the long trek, and to remain in good health. The climb itself was nothing short of miraculous. We were only four days off my most optimistic logistics plan; no one was hurt; we had just the right amount of gear and food; and the weather, for all of its threatening at a critical time, held off just long enough for us to climb the mountain.

After my last letter to you, we continued to have those afternoon showers, but the big storm never really materialized. Maybe all my worrying about it did some good. Shari said she never was really concerned about the storms, and didn't see why I kept making a big fuss. But, of course, she is from the Northwest.

Finally, three days past schedule, Shari, Lucy, Susan, and Stacy set up Camp III on the glacier. Once they arrived there, I knew we would get at least two people up and that I no longer needed to worry about the team making the summit. The rest of us moved up to Camp II and we were able to watch the others through binoculars all day as they climbed towards the summit. They seemed to take forever to inch their way up the snowfields, but we finally saw them disappear onto the summit about 3:30 P.M. Then, of course, all we had to worry about was their getting down safely. We had an especially heavy storm that evening, and I finally went to bed at 8:30 with the radio on, anxiously awaiting a call. I could imagine them out in the dark, being coated by the snow, headlamps searching into the void below, slowly and meticulously setting up their rappel anchors and easing themselves down. I hate rapeling in the dark, and I didn't envy them the chore even though it was a result of having reached the summit. Finally, at 9:20, Shari came on the radio to announce they were all tired but safe.

Then for the first time on the trip, I felt free to worry only about myself and my ambitions. As an expedition, we were now a success, having placed some climbers on the summit. Therefore any decisions I made in the next few days would no longer affect this success, and would only affect my own personal achievement of reaching the top.

We went up to Camp III the next day, passing the other four on their way down. The day was clear, with no snow, and I took that as a good omen. The first team members looked tired and sunburned, but quietly pleased with themselves. They told us the climbing wasn't difficult, just long, and I mentally girded myself for the physical effort it would entail, trying to regain some personal drive and ambition for the summit. I felt I was just drifting along on the impetus created by the others, aiming for a goal that was a reality for me.

We were up at 3 A.M. the next morning, determined to get going before daybreak. Molly, you've done enough morning starts with me to know what a joy I am before 10 A.M., but I found myself beginning to get excited at last, and I had no trouble rousing myself in time and even eating some awful granola. After the usual wrestling match (four people stuffed into one tent trying to get dressed into the correct clothing without putting an elbow into their neighbor's eye), I stumbled out the door and began buckling on my technical gear. The night sky was dotted with brilliant stars that cast enough starlight to illuminate all the mountains around us and leave the valleys below in shadow. For me, early dawn is such a mystical time to be on a mountain, knowing that the world is asleep at my feet, and knowing that I am about to go where few people ever go. I enjoy that feeling of isolation from the rest of the world, with a single clear goal before me; that paradox of total self-sufficiency yet dependence on my climbing partner.

We finally moved out about 5 A.M., and worked our way up the firm, frozen snow. The climb was basically easy, and we moved along steadily. Unfortunately, clear weather was not our fate. We climbed into thickening fog and snow as we gained altitude, and became totally socked in by 11 A.M. Anne and I reached the summit about 1:15, with Heidi and Jini arriving an hour later. By then it was snowing heavily and we dashed off back down. I was not excited about being on the summit. It looked like any other snowfield in a snow storm. Mostly, I was just glad to be finished moving upward.

We got back to Camp III about 7 P.M. after two rappels in the dark. Thank goodness the first team had marked their rappel anchors--nothing like looking for a little red flag waving in the dark trying to signal you to its haven of security.

The next day we took down the camp and retreated to Camp II and into the worse storm of the climb. My vacation from responsibility was over. As I went down, I could feel myself beginning to reluctantly take on again the cloud of decisions yet to be made to finish the climb: how to safely clear equipment off the mountain, who would be strong enough to help, how to get everything packed up for the return to Kathmandu, what to pay the Sherpas and how much of a bonus to give them, how much cash we would need to clear our debts in Nepal. But, I knew that we had succeeded in my ultimate desire--a Sherpaless ascent of a big, technical mountain with everyone reaching the summit. So worries such as these seemed small.

When we finish all of these details and officially end the expedition, Anne, Shari, Lucy and I are going up to the Everest Basecamp to take a look at the West Ridge. Anne is on an expedition to climb that route in the fall of 1983 and Shari, Lucy and I are considering applying to become team members. It will be fun to travel just as four friends, each of us responsible only for ourselves, and I look forward to the excitement of seeing a part of Nepal new to me.

My perception of events on this climb has been so different from climbs where I was just a team member that I hope I never lead another one. I don't like the feeling of isolation and detachment I have felt on this trip, and I doubt that I could ever change my nagging demand for perfection in details that causes me so much anguish at times. Oh, to be a peon again, to be responsible for only one job, to be answerable for only my own ambitions and desires! I look forward on my next trip to losing myself in the anonymity of being "one of the gang" again.

Aug. 5, 1982

Dear Molly,
Your letter finally caught up with me, the one you sent to Nepal last April that I never received because I had already left the country. It arrived like a ghost from the past, asking all those questions and making all those comments months after our return. But with the perspectives of time, I find I can better answer some of those questions and better understand my feelings about the trip.

As I think I mentioned in some of my letters, I found being the leader a mixed blessing. When I accepted the leadership from Annie, I did so reluctantly, because I felt I didn't have enough experience to lead an expedition to a high mountain. But I wanted to climb Ama Dablam and I wasn't sure I could get on the trip if someone else became the leader. So I accepted figuring I could learn as I went along.

I must admit my ego didn't mind all those times I could say I was The Leader--the title always seems so impressive. In Nepal it definitely carried political and social clout, and I would get to (have to?) stand with the big names at any functions. For example, we had dinner at our sirdar's house in Namche Bazaar, and we were all given katas (white scarves given to guests as a sign of respect). The others all received the standard gauze ones, but I got a big silk one, just because I was the leader. I was even given a fancy teacup, especially for me. But as I discovered during the climb, these perks carry a price. I definitely felt isolated from the rest of the team, and this detachment detracted from my enjoyment of the trip. In fact, even now, months after the trip, I still don't know how the rest of the team feels about the climb. What do they tell their friends about their experience on the mountain? Did they have a good time? Did the trip go as they expected? I can guess what some of them would answer, but I still am not sure.

When people ask me how I feel about the success of the climb, getting everyone to the summit, I say I'm very pleased. But inside, there's a part of me that does not feel that success. Because I did no technical lead climbing, I feel as though I climbed the mountain through the efforts of the others. All I had to do was jumar the lines the others put in; I didn't really earn the summit. I can't even answer the question, "Was it hard?" Jumaring is just physical labor, and does not reveal if the leading was difficult. I know this is an irrational feeling, but it still detracts from my own personal sense of achievement.

And yet, for all these feelings, I basically had a very good time on the trip. I am still astonished at how smoothly it went, which I attribute in large measure to the experience and competence of the team. We all kept commenting on how little we had to say in our diaries, and that they were boring because of the lack of conflict to write about. Certainly we had some personal confrontations but they were minor compared to what I've seen (and read about) on other trips. In fact, Shari, Lucy and I decided to join Anne on the trip to Everest in '83. Having tasted the power of being Leader, it may be hard to become just a team member again, but somehow I think I will be quite happy to join the gang and creatively second-guess the leader's decisions without having to pay a penalty for a mistake. Besides, I need all the summit drive I can muster if I hope to climb Everest.

Sue

Sue Giller is one of America's best female mountaineers. She has been part of three Everest expeditions, member of the all woman Dhaulaguri and Ama Dablam expeditions. She is a member of the American Alpine Club. She holds a B. A. degree in chemistry from the University of Illinois and has done graduate work in analytic chemistry at M.I.T. Sue is currently employed as a computer programmer, writing statistical programs.

The Other Love
Linda Givler

Fifteen years ago I found the man with whom I wanted to share the rest of my life.

He was the most loving, wonderful human being that one could ever hope to meet. I didn't think at the time that perhaps our happiness had to do with two people interacting--I was very young and all I could see was strength and male beauty and kindness and FINALLY someone who really loved me and allowed me to express my feelings and returned my love without any restrictions. I gave myself completely to this person, shared my most intimate thoughts with him, and planned our lives together for ever and always, even taking vows that ended in "*til death do us part.*" I shared this wonderful man with only one other woman.

I knew that I was as important to him as he was to me, but always in the background loomed that OTHER WOMAN, always there waiting for her turn to have him. And rather than resenting her, I too loved her. Sometimes we went to her together, and spent lovely days in the MOUNTAINS where this woman/mountain goddess lives. I felt that it was fair for him to visit her for periods of time, sometimes to teach a class of aspiring mountaineers, and sometimes to stay with her for the duration of an expedition to reach the top of a peak. But it was understood that she would always return him to me. That she would share this man who loved the high places. But, she cheated . . . she became greedy and she had to keep him for herself. Now I am alone, my dreams are dissolving and life has been very bleak indeed.

My husband was killed in a climbing accident ten years ago. It has been a long, difficult struggle to finally accept that he is gone, and that I am still here and that it is OK for me to continue living my life. And more important, that I can be happy again. Women, more than men, have traditionally had to deal with living as survivors. Men go to battle in one form or another, and often they do not come home. Women in the mountaineering community have recently begun to participate in more difficult and therefore more dangerous activities, but by and large more men than women venture off on trips of exteme difficulty. How does a woman learn to cope with the idea that her loved one may not come home from some trip, and what happens to her if that becomes a reality? I had been very aware of the possibility of Al Givler dying in the mountains, but like most of us, did not imagine for an instant that it would ever come to be. I still remember all too well the words that my dear friend said to me that day in June of 1977, "Linda, Dusan and Al won't be coming home" ... so simply put, words that told me nothing yet found their way into my very inner self and triggered something inside of me that I did not know existed. From somewhere deep within me and from some place in the past of women who have experienced this before me came a scream of anguish that symbolized all that I felt then and in the years to come. I found it very comforting to have Louise Sumner there with me at this moment of first impact, but even then, in that indescribable state of mind, I wondered why she came forward from the group to tell me, and why the two men stayed in the background. Louise later told me that she felt she was strong enough to handle this situation; but she, too, has been haunted all of these years by the scream of sorrow and the silent plea that asked that this not be possible.

During the first few months that followed, Diana Jagerska--the wife of the second victim, Dusan Jagersky--and I became inseparable. It was strangely comforting to have another person who was experiencing the same agony with whom to share this sorrow. There was so much to do at first. We flew to Alaska, to Glacier Bay where the accident occured, and brought with us climbing packs and gear so that we could go up to the mountain and bring these two "bad boys" home because, after all, the others must be wrong and really they were still alive. Flying into Glacier Bay National Monument and seeing the flag at half mast did not deter our thinking in the least little bit. "It's a holiday," I explained to Diana, "they always put the flag at half mast on holidays." Louise and Bill Sumner, who were accompanying us, must have been astounded at our thought process during this trip. Even when we saw Jim Wickwire and Steve Marts, the other two climbers--the survivors--and Jim and Lou Whittaker who had come up on their own to help search for the bodies, still we did not believe. Maybe the sight of the person with the black bag triggered something in me; it was then that I realized that he had in there small pieces of skin and bones and hair that used to be those two wonderful, very alive, human beings who should have been there, too. It seems you have to have such proof to issue a death certificate. We stayed in Glacier Bay for a few days, I think, and we were able to fly around the peak that robbed me of my reason for living. Even now I had to see that this was indeed a beautiful peak, I loved to look at it, I could feel the sense of excitement that they must have had to be the first ones to stand on her summit and feel that incredible sense of accomplishment at having achieved their goal. Then we flew around to the descent and I saw the four thousand foot drop that Al and Dusan went over, and this mountain goddess looked evil and menacing and it made me feel very angry that the place where they ended up was so forlorn looking. How odd a thought, really--does the spirit stay inside the body? I think not.

We returned home to Seattle. The rest of the City went back to living their usual lives, doing everyday things. For me it became an excruciating exercise to force myself out of bed in the morning. What was the point? For a while there were things to be done: arranging this and that, a memorial service which we held at Mt. Rainier National Park, the retrieval of the gear that had been left at base camp, writing to people who sent condolences, and the first viewing of the movie that Steve Marts made of the climb. Then what . . . . I returned to my summer job as a backcountry ranger, thinking that being in the mountains would be soothing and make me feel closer to Al. Fortunately, my friends took it to heart to spend time with me and seemed to have put together some network whereby, as one group hiked out, another group came into my camp and therefore I was not left alone in the woods. At the time it seemed very mysterious, but I later learned to appreciate this wonderful thoughtfulness.

Summer ended and I returned to the University to attempt to finish my studies in Forestry. That, too, had less meaning for me now. Al and I had planned that, during the summers, he would teach and guide while I worked as a backcountry ranger or perhaps helped instruct climbing. Reality began to creep back closer to me and I had to think about how in the world I was going to support myself on three months of work each year. It began to seem like I had to think seriously about planning a new future, even though I had no interest in thinking about such a thing if it meant planning a life alone.

The mountaineering community is a close knit group of people. This had been most comforting to both Diana and myself for about one year after Al and Dusan disappeared. However, we began to feel that perhaps we were being watched all too closely and that it might be time to try to find out what living was like again. In order for each of us to accomplish these goals, we had to get away from Seattle, our families, friends, and the memories that were everywhere we went. She left to be the base camp manager of the 1978 K-2 expedition, and I went to Grand Teton National Park in Wyoming to spend a summer as a ranger.

I felt that I wanted to try to live again, and I knew that I was excruciatingly lonely for my husband. Since it was beginning to seem like he wasn't going to be back for a long, long, time, I decided that I might allow myself to associate with other men. This was a very difficult decision to make. What I really wanted to do was to find someone as much like Al as possible and then mold him into a replica so that my loss would not be so intense. Along with this yet unknown inner desire was the guilt I had for even thinking that I could be interested in another man. All of this made for very interesting encounters. I found that I really had become incapable of entering into another committed relationship and searched out men who were also unable to sustain a long term affair.

What does all of this mean to people who climb? We know that it is a dangerous activity and the chances of an accident occuring are great. Does it make any difference if you are the person going or the person staying home? Will it make any difference when choosing a new partner if you have once experienced this loss to the mountain goddess? I don't think so. What I do see is that this is a subject that appears to be forbidden territory for many climbers. I don't believe that most of us want to admit that death is around us and may creep into our lives against our will. I have never heard of a group of people, other than those who have experienced the death of a family member, talking about the risk that is run each time one or both people venture out to do a climb. It's usually an unspoken arrangement. People marry, have children, and suddenly one or both of them no longer do difficult climbs. Occasionally, my men friends have commented on this subject and admitted that it would be too horrible a thought to imagine leaving behind a wife and children. But they don't say anything more than that. Most of us don't talk about it or admit that the fear is there, because we can't go on climbing if we are afraid. One must always approach the snow or rock with a positive attitude, and know and believe that you will return and once again cheat death. More than talking seriously about the consequences of a bad fall, we tell rotten jokes about how we managed to return home all in one piece. It's hard, if not impossible, to match the thrill that you get from completing a hard climb. And with that physical challenge is the mental one that allows you to fully concentrate on one goal and keep your cool while doing it. Do we ever think about the one who is at home waiting and waiting while someone else is up at 26,000' or maybe only at 1,000' but it's hard climbing and it is dangerous.

Sure, people do think about the ones left behind, but that doesn't stop this burning desire to go out and climb ever more difficult routes or peaks.

I have lived with grief and pain for a long time now, and I have just recently been able to understand and accept what has happened to me. This may seem incredible to most people but it happened and it will continue to happen to others. You can't rush overcoming a loss. I don't feel anger at the mountains, I have no intention to quit climbing; quite obviously if this were the case, it would have occured a long time ago. I'd just like to be able to explain to others that it does get better. For those who do not climb, who have never felt the wonder and awe when seeing such incredible beauty or the rush of exhilaration when completing a physically difficult portion of a climb it always sounds so stupid to tell them that it was worth it to the one who is gone. To those of us at home--left behind to continue our daily lives--those who died in the mountains have gone to a new territory and we should not be mourning for them. Our grief and sorrow is mostly for our own selves. I know I did not want to live alone. I still do not. But I won't pick a non-climber out of the crowd and I won't give it up myself. It's an addiction. We are far worse off than any drug addict could ever imagine. Our curse takes us to physical and mental highs and satisfies some urge to challenge ourselves. We feel healthy and happy and we don't see that it could ever be wrong to do what we do.

Linda Givler has been involved in all aspects of climbing since the early 1970's. She has climbed extensively in the northwest including some trips to South America and to the Karakorum. Linda attended the school of forestry at the University of Washington and has worked as a back country ranger in both Grand Teton and Mount Rainier National Parks. Currently she manages Great Pacific Patagonia in Seattle.

Linda Givler

Walls Without Balls
Sibylle C. Hectell

Memories of a California climber during the 70's

When asked to write about women climbing in California during the 1970's, I thought, "Aha, another chance to use this title." I used it for an article I wrote for the American Alpine Journal in 1974. Ad Carter, the editor, wrote that he loved the title, but that the board of directors would not permit its use. They preferred "Keeping Abreast on El Cap." I sent back an indignant letter on the suitability of female body parts in a title, while male body parts were taboo. Insistence on my title resulted in the publication of "Untitled" (AAJ, 1974).

This censorship indicates the prevailing attitudes at that time. The climbing power elite fifteen years ago were officious, pompous men who weren't about to tolerate irreverence toward the established institutions, especially from a woman.

The attitudes of women climbers, and their expectations, have also changed tremendously from 1970 to the 80's. The high standard at which women are climbing today demonstrates that we have the ability to do hard routes. If few women were doing these twenty years ago, it was ideas which were the limiting factor, not physical ability.

WHY SO FEW WOMEN?

There were always isolated instances of women climbing with men, usually husbands or guides. There were rare instances of all-female ascents throughout the history of mountaineering. Until recently, however, women climbers were rare and all-female ascents an even greater anomaly.

There were many reasons for this. Social barriers were significant. In *CLIMBING IN NORTH AMERICA,* Chris Jones notes that in 1909 women had to be far from camp before they were permitted to "unhitch their voluminous skirts and reveal the racy climbing knickerbockers underneath." Prior to the women's liberation movement of the 1960's and the accompanying loosening of sexual mores, it was difficult for women to go on climbs with men that involved overnight trips (and they certainly couldn't live in Camp 4).

Psychological barriers were a second problem. Monica Jackson, in the BOOK OF MODERN MOUNTAINEERING (1968), says that "the myth persists that women who mountaineer seriously must be over-masculine or sexually frustrated.... There is still a good deal of remarkably reactionary suspicion of woman mountaineers floating around among male climbers, which makes any breakthrough by the women considerably more difficult." She concludes that women should be included on international expeditions because "there is no reason why they should not have done as well as their male colleagues, (and) think how much more amusing the subsequent books about the expeditions would have been."

A third reason there were few women climbing was that few women before the 1980's participated in any sport whatsoever. Many women who have taken up climbing recently have athletic backgrounds--downhill ski racing, swimming, running, and cross country skiing. Lynn Hill and Bev Johnson are both former gymnasts. Before the mid-1960's, few women had participated in another sport long enough to retire from it to rock climbing.

ON THE LEAD

Before 1980, a woman leading hard climbs was so rare that when she led 5.10, it was recorded in the climbing journals. Historically, men didn't lead climbs either - guides did. At an 1870 Alpine Club meeting, it was decided that "neglect to take guides on difficult expeditions ... is totally unjustifiable and calculated to produce the most lamentable results." "Guideless" climbing constituted a minor revolution, occurring between 1880 and 1930. The first "manless ascents" followed soon thereafter. However, women climbers and female teams remained rare until 1960.

The small number of women climbing is a factor often overlooked when explaining why so few women led 5.10 in 1970. By 1971 I climbed in Oregon, Washington, Canada, New Hampshire and California, as well as climbing in Europe as a child. My parents were both climbers. Since they had no son, it was obvious that I would follow in my father's bootprints. My father, who still climbs hard 5.10 at 73, had done many first ascents in the Alps and led expeditions to South America and the Himalayas. In his weekends at home, he took me climbing.

I saw no other women climbing until I went to Yosemite in September, 1971. There, I met three women climbers-Bev Johnson, Anne Marie Rizzi, and Judy Sterner, and heard about a fourth-Elaine Matthews. Of the four, two led 5.10. What a change -for a year and a half I never saw another female climber. Now that I had met some, they all seemed to be superwomen. It was both inspiring and intimidating.

Originally a southern debutante, Beverly Johnson had gone to Kent State on a gymnastics scholarship and then transferred to USC in Los Angeles. When I met her, she was the temporary park ranger in charge of fee collection at Camp 4 - a job the park service didn't usually hire climbers for. Bev was leading some very difficult routes, including New Dimensions, the first 5.11 in Yosemite. She had also done the NW Face of Half Dome and the Chouinard-Herbert Route on Sentinel Dome. She was particularly strong in off-width cracks and flaring, awkward chimneys, as I was sorry to learn (I wasn't).

Anne Marie Rizzi and Judy Sterner were both Californians. Anne Marie was from the San Fernando Valley and worked for Curry Company. Living in Yosemite was her introduction to climbing. Judy was from the Bay Area and had been introduced to mountain climbing through the active Bay Area Climbing community. Neither had climbed very long, but both were solid 5.9 leaders. Anne Marie climbed the Chouinard-Herbert Route on Sentinel that year, and Judy went to Canada and became an outstanding mountaineer.

Elaine Matthews was a legend. She had led the hardest climbs of any woman, including the West Face of Sentinel. In 1970, she and Chuck Ostin swung leads up to Camp VI on the Nose, where they were rescued due to a blizzard. They would have reached the top with better weather: they had completed all the difficult free climbing, the hardest aid pitches, all the pendulums, and hauled the hardest part of the route. Elaine was infamous for her appearance as a nude cover girl for the Vulgarian Digest. She lived in New York, so I didn't meet her until a 1972 trip to the Wind Rivers, but the tales of her hard climbs were endless.

In fall 1972, I met one more female climber - Barbara Devine, who led 5.11, and I started leading my first few 5.10's (unknowingly, as they were still rated 5.9 at the time). It is difficult to pinpoint the precise moment when women began climbing 5.11, or even 5.10, because often we didn't realize we were doing it. I led my first 5.10's, and followed and led my first 5.11's all without realizing I had ever done so. Ratings in the 5.10 range were rather tenuous after the establishment of the first 5.11 in 1970. Bev remarked, "Bridwell likes to take me along on first ascents. If I get up, it's 5.10, and if I don't it's 5.11."

The first 5.11, New Dimensions, was put up in 1970 by Jim Bridwell and Mark Klemens. By 1974, four women I knew led 5.11 (Johnson, Devine, Hechtel, and Hunter) and most likely others I didn't know. Diana Hunter led Wide Country (5.11) along with many other difficult climbs in Colorado and Yosemite, but they were still rated 5.10 at the time. In spring 1974, I led Rebolting Development at Suicide Rock, which was 5.10 in the existing guide, and Season's End, which wasn't in the guide. They are both rated 5.11 now. Although we were not at the forefront of rock climbing, we were close.

Despite this, the prejudices against women still existed, and they consisted of more than mild disapproval. Some men just would not relinquish the lead. In September 1971, I went to Yosemite and met a German climber, Heinrich. We decided to try Point Beyond, a 5.7. I was intimidated by Yosemite and expected 5.7's here to be harder than elsewhere. Heinrich assured me that he would lead everything. Despite this I was surprised when he insisted on leading the two 5.1 pitches up Monday Morning Slab. When I offered to lead, he said that he was the leader.

He continued up the first two pitches of Point Beyond. After failing on the third pitch, he decided we would have to rappel. I asked again if I could try the pitch. He finally agreed, though he was convinced I had no chance of getting up it. Unable to second the pitch, he pendulumed across the crux traverse. After this, he let me swing leads on our climbs.

A year later, my father asked me to climb with his German friend Bruno Friedrich, who spoke no English and was heading to the Valley. I'd just been snowed on in the Wind Rivers, so September in Yosemite seemed a pleasant alternative. I wasn't ready for Bruno's enthusiasm: I flailed up a number of hard off-widths and 5.10 chimneys with him, and by mid-September we were on the NW Face of Half Dome.

This was not something I planned on. I hadn't led much aid, jumared much, and had never hauled. I also didn't have any choice in the matter. Bruno was in Yosemite for four weeks, spoke no English, had no climbing partner, and was determined to be the first German up Half Dome (by default, I became the second German up it).

Bruno led the hard pitches, I led the easy ones, and I learned a lot about walls. Best of all, I discovered that I enjoyed doing walls. Half Dome is a great place to start, because there are lovely, flat ledges spaced at the right intervals. I loved waking up in the morning, watching the sunrise from my bag, and turning my head enough to peek over the edge, 2000' straight down at tiny trees and rivers, the glory of the Valley spread out before me.

BIG WALLS

1973 was an auspicious year for women climbers in Yosemite. We began to reach critical mass and activity fermented. Women from Washington, Julie Brugger, Catherine Freer, Carla Firey, passed through the Valley and Barbara Devine from the Gunks had paid a visit. In 1973 we had the strongest and most numerous resident contingent ever. In addition to Bev, Anne Marie, and myself, Diana Hunter from Colorado and Ellie Hawkins, also from Washington, were living in the Valley.

Bev Johnson began the year on an appropriate note by soloing the South Face of Washington Column. Diana Hunter burst into fervent free climbing. My second route of the year was Stone Groove, with Diana and Jim Donini. Diana then swung leads on the DNB, presaging the brilliant face climbing she later put to use in leading Wide Country (5.11) in Eldorado Canyon. Her tragic death in 1975 was not only a personal loss but a setback for the climbing community as a whole.

Anne-Marie Rizzi and I took off a weekend from our busy college schedule to climb Washington Column. Everything that could go wrong did - severe lightning storms, heat, illness, general incompetence - so we didn't quite make it in a weekend.

I spent the summer climbing in the Bugaboos and Canadian Rockies. When I returned I learned that Bev had climbed the Nose with Dan Asay. Anne Marie had a horrible time on Half Dome (brilliantly described in her article) and had sold or given away her climbing gear. I did various short routes with both Bev and Ellie and noticed that Bev was sending me up on hard leads and carefully interrogating my climbing partners. When she suggested that I climb the Leaning Tower to get used to overhanging aid, I began to suspect her motives. Slowly it dawned on me that Bev was looking for an El Cap accomplice.

At the time, I was dubious about this, being a relative novice at climbing and also a busy student. Bev however had her plans firmly in mind and only needed an accomplice. Once again, by elimination, I was it. Anne Marie had quit climbing, Ellie had prior plans with her husband, and I was the only other woman with any wall experience. I took her advice and climbed the Leaning Tower with Roy Naasz. We made it up in the usual time and manner. After quizzing Roy carefully, she decided we were ready for El Cap.

There were other reasons for us to get off the Valley floor. Climbers tend to move around. Bev had lived in Squaw Valley for the winter, and had two boy friends, one of whom was usually in the East Coast and the second in Mammoth. By an unfortunate coincidence, they both arrived in the Valley simultaneously.

I had the opposite problem. I was madly infatuated with Walter Rosenthal, whose tent I had been inhabiting part-time. Walter decided that he would solo the Dihedral Wall and had no time for female distractions. He replaced me with a large rack of hardware and bivvy food, spread about the tent floor, and explained that he needed to concentrate on his impending solo. I decided that if he wouldn't see me because he was climbing El Cap, then I'd show him and go climb it myself. Bev and I set out on the Triple Direct on the same day that Walter started up the Dihedral.

We chose the Triple Direct because it was the easiest route. Robbins described it as a "bastard route" lacking in personality, but our first priority was to get to the top. We both lived in Camp 4, Bev was on the rescue squad, and we knew that a failure of the first women's attempt on El Cap would be a fiasco we could never live down. With this firmly in mind we took equipment for all contingencies: extra water, rainflies, storm gear, and an extra hammer in the bottom of the haul bag. No wonder the damn thing weighed over a hundred pounds.

At Mammoth Terrace, we left the Salathe route and headed up and right to join the Muir. This was as far as our topographical map went, and we got lost off of Block Ledge. Bev tried going straight up, plus up and left, and then started yelling for Charlie Porter at the top of her lungs. I was rather surprised until she explained that Charlie's van was right down below, that Charlie had just done the Shield, and that he could tell us which way to go. Charlie heard us, but we could never hear him. Luckily the one remaining direction, up and right, got us on route.

Walls Without Balls

Climbing proceeded well up to the top of the Muir corners. Leading out right onto the prow on an easy bolt ladder was spectacular. We had been inside huge corners, protected from wind and exposure. Suddenly I was out on the prow. Wind rushed by me, and I could see around to the other side of the immense wall we were inching up. It was one of the most incredible sights I had ever seen. Then the bolts ended. Mystified, I looked up for cracks, pin holes, anything--was I supposed to hook across this?

"Bev, the bolts end. I don't have any hooks." An evil cackling came from behind the corner.

"Pendulum!"

Oh, of course, pendulum. This was a good place to learn.

"I've never done a pendulum before!" I wailed.

Bev was as reassuring as usual. "It's easy. I'll lower you. Just run back and forth. Be careful nailing at the end, that's an expanding flake."

I was clearly headed to my doom. Here I was, 2000' off the ground, about to run back and forth to nail my first "expanding flake." I wasn't ready for this, but penduluming actually turned out to be fun, once I got over being scared. I made it past the dread flake using nuts.

We soon reached Camp 4 on the Nose, decided it looked uncomfortable, and headed off towards Camp 5. We reached Camp 5 in the dark, Bev unpacking the haul bag and eating by headlamp while I cleaned in the dark. What an oversight not to borrow a second headlamp - we'd already borrowed pins, biners, jumars, hardware slings, a sit harness, bivvy gear, hammer, and pulleys.

I've always loved bivvies on walls - watching headlamps twinkling on Middle Cathedral, watching the moon rise over Half Dome and looking at the sculptured beauty of El Cap. It's just as well I liked them, because we had one more. The next day, we equivocated on reaching Camp 6 and then decided to go for the top. We didn't make it. We sat on small footholds, until I discovered that one can sleep by putting one's butt in a belay seat, head in one ertrier, and feet in the second ertrier. In the morning, Bev complained bitterly that whenever she tried to talk to me, I was asleep. A little stiff, we stuffed our gear in the bag and took off for the top, just a few pitches away.

That same month, Ellie Hawkins climbed the Salathe Wall with her husband Bruce and Keith Nannery. I sat in El Cap meadows, watching her lead the third pitch - the hardest nailing on the route. The story was that she went up because she was 100 pounds lighter than her partners and had fewer chances of pulling the pins. It was an impressive accomplishment. Ellie was lucky though - she didn't have to do any hauling. In October, 1973, Bev went back up on El Cap with Charlie Porter to do the first ascent of Grape Race. Altogether, 1973 saw a total of 5 woman-ascents of El Cap, three of them by the indomitable Beverly Johnson.

After a lull in 1974, I climbed the Salathe in fall 1975, with Tom Dunwiddie and Alec Sharp. In 1976, Molly Higgins from Colorado climbed the Nose with Barb Eastman. This was the first all-woman ascent of the Nose and the second of El Cap. By now there had been nine attempts by women to climb El Cap, eight of which were successful. Ironically, the only failed attempt was the first, that by Elaine Matthews.

Perhaps my friend Dave Evans remembered these statistics in September 1977. I was in Orange County, working on my Ph.D. when he drove down from Yosemite and insisted that I return with him to climb the Nose. As always, I was a pushover for being talked into anyone else's insane climbing ideas. This one was ok, except that Dave insisted that we under no circumstances use hammers. To avoid temptation we would leave them on the ground. My protest that hammers were useful for testing fixed pins, and that the party of three which had recently fallen off of Dolt Tower was rumored to have pulled a bolt were of no avail.

It seemed that I got all the pitches that were hard to do without pins. The offwidth before Dolt Tower was mine. Bridwell had said, "Don't worry, it's a piece of cake. Just layback it." Easy for him to say. I remembered something vague about Charles Cole having leapfrogged #10 hexes. I tried that method and it worked. My next ordeal was leading Boot Flake with just a few of the correct size of hexentrics and stoppers (Friends hadn't been invented). Dave berated me for being too slow and suggested that I get off my ertriers and free-climb the rest. Somehow Dave was uninclined to follow his own free-climbing advice on Pancake Flake.

I led one more horror - a slimy slit that is utterly unprotectable with nuts. It wasn't mentioned as being difficult on any topo, I'd never heard of it, so I assumed it must be an easy free section and went for it. When we got down, Kevin and Tim Powell told us they'd thought Boot Flake was the hardest aid pitch on nuts and that Tim had backed off the slimy slot. I wondered, Tim aiding Boot Flake? He'd led 5.11's I couldn't follow. Dave decided I was possibly an acceptable climbing partner after all - we had gotten to the top in 3 1/2 days and without hammers. I decided I would never again listen to advice from any of my friends.

In 1978, Bev pulled off the ultimate coup: she soloed the Dihedral Wall. Now she had done it all: the first female ascent, the first all-female ascent, the first woman on a first ascent, and the first woman to solo El Cap. There's not much left except an all-female new route and a female solo first ascent.

CHANGING ATTITUDES: VERSION 2

Women's expectations of themselves and their predominantly male climbing partners changed as much as men's expectations of women climbers. Goals have changed greatly. My goals at the beginning of summer 1971 were to lead 5.6 and follow 5.7. I doubt any woman who starts climbing today would have such modest ambitions. Today many women lead 5.11, some lead 5.12, and it is widely publicized.

As women accomplished more, men's attitudes toward and expectations of, women change concommitantly. Today, if I go to a climbing area alone and ask a man if he'll climb with me, he usually asks what I can lead. Fifteen years ago a more likely response was the question, "I guess, what can you follow?"

Most of the changes in women's climbing over the last fifteen years have been positive. There are more women climbing, they are accepted as equals and are in an environment more conducive to their success. No longer is their right to lead climbs questioned.

Along with the benefits of a more supportive atmosphere comes one disadvantage: there is much more pressure today for women to push their limits, and to raise the standard of their climbing. This pressure is no different from that facing serious male climbers, but it is a pressure we didn't feel for a long time. In 1971 it never occurred to me that leading 5.7 was inadequate, and I had tremendous fun doing it. Today women start climbing 5.8's and advance to harder climbs within weeks. As this happens, they are suffering more stress-related injuries such as tendonitis and ligament problems (just like men). To most, it is a price worth paying.

Are the changes for the better? Is women's climbing today better than it was ten years ago? I don't think women had it better then, or now, just that our experiences are different. It was difficult for a woman climber to become accepted then, but once we were, it was terrific. I was able to climb almost everything I wanted, despite being female. I miss some older attitudes -- I liked never feeling any pressure to perform.

Many of the changes have benefitted both sexes. Today, men don't have to choose between staying home with their wives versus going climbing. They can go on a climbing trip together. I personally just realized an enormous benefit from the current focus on including women: I was invited on a climbing exchange to the U.S.S.R. The last exchange, in 1976, included no women. This trip, organized by the same person, was given a mandate that they must take women. I asked to go on the last one and they wouldn't consider it.

This year, they called me.

Sibylle C. Hechtel has been at the forefront of women's climbing for some time. She, along with the likes of Bev Johnson, Lynn Hill, Beth Bennett, Carla Firey and Julie Brugger, is responsible for pushing women's climbing standards past the 5.10 range. This group was also instrumental in leading the way for all female routes in Yosemite, JoshuaTree and El Dorado, not to mention many female solo routes.

A immigrant from Germany, Sibylle currently lives in Boulder, Colorado. She received a B.A. in zoology from U.C. Berkeley and a Ph.D. in biology from U.C. Irvine. She has taught at both Irvine and University of Michigan. Sibylle has also held a faculty research fellowship at the California Institute of Technology. She is currently doing research dealing with molecular evolution, cloning and DNA sequencing.

Sibylle has climbed extensively in the western U.S., Mexico and Canada.

In the winter season of 1984 Chris Chandler, M.D. and Cherie Bremer-Kamp made the first winter attempt of Kangcherjunga's North Face.

This was to be Cherie's 4th attempt on an 8,000 meter peak having climbed high on Dhaulagini, K2 and Yalangkong. All but K2 were 2-person teams without the use of supplemental O_2. Another look at K2 was planned the following summer.

There was every reason to be optimistic for success, perched in a shallow cave with the summit pyramid towering 2000 feet above. Yet fate would have it otherwise. Instead, Chris succumbed to a sudden and crippling onset of cerebral oedema. Mongol Sigg Tamang, their sherpa companion, and Cherie barely managed to get Chris down 1000 feet, where he died that night.

Frostbitten hypothermic and critically dehydrated, closer to death than life, Cherie and Mongol took four days to finally reach Base Camp.

Separated from her soul-mate by death, writing became a tool for investigating and understanding the pain that followed, using it as wisely as she dared.

> *"The Moving Finger writes; and, having writ,*
> *Moves on: nor all your Piety nor Wit*
> *Shall lure it back to cancel half a line, Nor all your*
> *Tears wash out a Word of it."*

Omar Khayyam

Horizons
Cherie Bremer Kamp

"And so, Cherie, have you thought about what your horizons are?" The voice echoed in the overly large room. A feeling grew at the base of my neck, creeping slowly through the hair follicles to concentrate on the very top of my head. What's he just done to me? The feeling filtered through my senses that I had been administered some mind altering drug. Oh God, he'll probably think I'm stoned. I glanced at the finely built man, dressed in a white polo neck sweater and kind smile, my psychiatrist.

"Horizons, did you say horizons?" He nodded in quiet approval. I laughed nervously at the feeling that enveloped me. I'd be so embarrassed if I lost it here right now. Wanting on one hand the safety of being 'normal' yet lured on to examine just a little longer that curiously raw feeling that lay beneath polite behavior and social graces. Words fell from my lips, obedient to form. I wavered, mid stream. Which shore to swim to? Or would the current's strength sweep me where it would?

Seconds flew by as I once more experienced the joy of climbing, the thrill and closeness with another human that I shared with Chris--looking out over those distant horizons . . . .

Too soon I realized I was facing a grey wall of granite. I had no need to look down. I knew they were there, those little stubs that remain of my fingers. How could they ever find a purchase on that grey, seemingly impenetrable wall of granite to move nimbly upwards into the clear blue sky?

And where had my friend and lover gone? I stood on the gound in a puddle of impotence, 'I don't see any horizons' I answered lamely.

Struggling in a headlong confrontation with destiny, I tried once more to throw off this feeling of despair that so drained my power and productivity.

It was vital to my survival to preserve the memory of the freedom I found so available in the mountains. To interrupt my everyday existence of running a household and earning a living and expose myself to cold, fatigue, isolation, and danger interspersed with long periods of confinement in storm-bound tents had a way of stripping away the superficial layers of life, allowing the freedom to look inward, to examine some of life's great mysteries.

It's observed when log fire and television set are available, most human beings will settle for that life. It is when basic needs are denied, and only then, that people are pushed to their essential depths of experience. Eating and sleeping are some of those most basic needs, and manipulating these needs by stringent rules of fasting and sleep deprivation have been used for centuries to gain insight into Religious truths.

Climbing encompasses that concept of grasping the meaning of life through certain crucial experiences: the death and grief of war, accidents, passionate loves, or great catastrophies of earthquakes and volcanic eruptions. The 'clamity theory' is that people evolve through conflict and struggle. Having led the adventurous life--survived the battleground, debilitating illness or earthquake that wrenched us into awareness--we could be now free to sit back in what may easily become smug complacency, or on the other hand, lured once more to taste the drug of action, as both opiate and stimulant.

Thrill is thought of as a fine tremor; an intense feeling of ecstasy but the word more obliquely can be used as 'to piece, penetrate, or cut through.' Need we ask why climbers climb, and at such great cost?

By studying the concepts of Hindu philosophy as found in the Vedas and Upanishads, we are promised a teaching which cuts through illusion. Perhaps we need not continue in a life of great exploits until death or fear overcomes us, only to be recalled in old age or graveside obituary. Even so, the way of life of a yogi ascetic is not too different from that of a himalayan alpinist. The simplicity of purpose, paucity of tools, isolation and deprivation blend. Whereas the yogi seeks 'non-action' as a vital meditative tool, the climber has it imposed upon him by the forces of nature pinned down for days or weeks on end by fierce storms, clinging to a small foothold on the edge of existence. In both cases, hardship and deprivation have stripped the ego bare. The mind is now set free to do its necessary work.

Two years ago this winter, Chris and I stood beneath Kanchenjunga's North Face. Today, alone, I face despair. I need to keep in check the impulse to drown out the screaming pain with so many readily available anaesthetics. Despair is not necessarily such a bad thing, for when all hope is gone, there is no fear. From that deep despair, a beauty is born and new possibilities can arise.

The idea of freedom that is born from despair is that one may not be able to do anything to alter the situation or set of circumstances that makes one a powerless victim of destiny. The release of power and freedom comes by developing the ability to change the context in how we view a particular situation. In other words, acceptance of fate without becoming fatalistic.

This is a continually difficult idea that I struggle with. Several months before the expedition was to leave San Francisco for our second alpine style attempt in Kanchenjunga's North Face in far eastern Nepal, our base camp manager Lori came to me with an urgent request. She needed to tell me about a dream she'd had. We both had just completed a hectic night shift in an intensive care unit and my emotional energy was drained. More from politeness than interest, I gave in to her request. With her eyes forcused on some place far from where she stood, she began to describe a scene of three people on a mountainside. It wasn't clear if they had reached the summit or not. One person sat alone close to some rocks looking on, almost as though he was guiding the efforts of the other two who were climbing down very slowly. She broke the narrative, twisting her facial muscles up in intense concentration. One person was yelling at the other who seemed hesitant and unsure of himself. There was a problem communicating, almost like a language barrier, and something was terribly wrong.

To this point, I had shown patience, but now I broke free of her grasp on my arm. I'd heard enough. Why implant subconscious messages on my brain--that Chris and I would be out of harmony on the mountain? I was acutely sensitive to the 'problems' in our relationship that usually arose from frustrated effort, yet these problems had a way of dissipating in our shared passion of climbing.

I dismissed the incongruity of three people instead of two on the mountain to some Freudian symbology of an 'alter ego.' From the moment of conception, the climb had always been a two-person attempt. She had caught my initial interest and attention, now it had gone too far. As I walked away, her voice trailed after me "there will be much falling."

"So, do we live or do we die?" I responded sardonically.

"That won't be known until the very last moment." I had pressed the button to the elevator and waited impatiently, but she insisted on continuing. "Cherie, you've got to do something about your hands, promise me. Your gloves . . . you lose one or drop one." I assured her that we always took an entire wardrobe of extra gloves along and that if anything froze, it would most likely be my feet. Finally, the elevator door opened, I stepped in, the door closed. I had escaped . . . or so I had thought. I never mentioned the incident to Chris.

It was hard enough wading through the mire of anxiety that our friends and loved ones often unwittingly projected at the beginning of a big trip, and I couldn't spend time on what I considered simply environmental noise. I had difficulty enough sorting through my own mental static and I did not want to add to Chris'. Usually it would take until we reached the flanks of a mountain, perhaps in the chill of an early morning sunrise to make that important connection with those inner feelings. I could be patient.

Hectic preparations for the trip soon overwhelmed us and the memory of the dream faded, until the night of January 5, 1985. I lay on a small platform that had been hacked out of hard winter snow. Mongol, our sherpa companion, lay on a similar one, a few feet to the left, and the body of Chris several feet below. My hands, although frozen into rigid claws, remained precious. I cradled them against my cheeks. My wooden legs lay in urine soaked down. I had litttle expectation of surviving the bitter cold of night. Overcome with grief and despair, I stared up into the abyssmal blackness of the night sky. Only then did I remember the dream and its significance in our present situation. Calm and peace replaced crippling fear and cold. Although it was still 'unknown' if Mongol and I were to survive the descent or not, I was no longer afraid and faced what lay ahead with calm acceptance.

Today I ponder that pivotal question. What was the purpose of Lori's dream? Given foreknowledge, how much could I have altered the course of events, if at all?

It is the exceptional person who does not retract from the possibility that our futures are fixed in cement, yet that night high on the side of Kanchenjunga, I marvelled at the unfolding events, the multiplicity of choices we discussed, each leading to an alternate future that could have replaced the one I was now experiencing.

No one can say that any event has 100% probability of occurring until all the conditions for its occurrence have been satisfied--and finally, that night, it had all fallen into place. Rather than reacting with horror at this realization, I was filled with perfect stillness, suspended by wonder of the universe.

It seemed important at the time that we take active part in vital decisions, to exercise our free-will that unwittingly led us on in what became a seemingly inescapable part of a greater cosmic design. Rollo May explains it such: "It is a paradox that destiny is significant only because a freedom of choice exists, that freedom being born from how we relate to our destiny. "

Skeptics representing the ultra-materialists could well argue my subconscious mind, open to suggestion, was "programmed" to run the course of events just as it was related in the dream. I doubt my cleverness at such self deceit and manipulation of events, and besides, what was my motive? Yet this remains an often quoted argument against fulfillment of prophecy. Unfortunately, the whole subject of precognition and distant viewing suffers credibility as much from "true believers" as it has from critics who have difficulty in accepting any scientific data on the subject. Yet the phenomenon is being regarded seriously enough by the governments of Russia and the U.S.A. to budget large amounts of dollars in carefully controlled experiments, the results of which were published in a congressional report in June, 1981, that suggest an interconnectedness of the human mind with other minds and matter, and implies the human mind is able to obtain information independent of geography and time.

So, if our lives are laid out before us in one Grand Design and our puerile calculations and awkward efforts do give into a higher plan, why should we not as Omar Khayyam suggest in the Rubaiyat--take the cup, drink the wine, and while away our time in licentius pleasures. Eastern philosophy's answer to how we should respond to this question is embraced by the concept of Karma.

Suppose there is an infinite variety of responses to one's Karma. It would depend on the quality of our thoughts as well as our actions with the consequence of either further enslavement in the wheel of suffering or release to final enlightenment. With Eastern philosophy blending with Rollo May's idea that our freedom is born from how we choose to relate to those events that make up our destiny, it seems the temptation to focus on manipulating the external events by peering into crystal balls, consulting oracles, or other methods could be better directed to the internal process of developing understanding and meaning from it. Nonetheless, it would be foolish to suggest crossing an avalanche prone slope when instincts and gut reactions cry out not to; or not to try to develop the ability to distinguish between mental clutter and valid intuitive, possibly life saving, information.

In situations such as skiing avalanche country or climbing big mountains where all the facts cannot be known, this sensitivity would seem a most valuable tool and something which Chris and I were at pains to develop. How then, could I have allowed such a powerful message as Lori's dream to slip by unrecognized, as well as all the other clear signs and messages and feelings pass unacknowledged? Or were they? Looking back, it seems as though there was a gigantic blockage between information given and information acted upon. What created that information block? A ready answer would be Blind Ambition and Presitge Seeking, but was that really it? If that was the prime motivating force, however much we denied it, surely we could have chosen a larger team with logistics that would ensure success.

We knew how small the odds were of our reaching the summit and it was a bit of a game to test them, always trusting that little voice inside to speak up when it was time to turn back. The summit was a goal and worth maybe the tip of a toe or two but not our lives. We often laughed about adding to our list of unsuccessful attempts. Mental stress was more likely responsible for interferring with our being in tune with our inner feelings. But to dissuade someone from going into the mountains because inherent stress might block hearing that voice within would be like recommending a diabetic not to take his insulin. The mountains were a place where stress was ameliorated rather than accumulated. Sometimes now, perhaps when coming across a forgotten photo of the climb, I recall unexplained feelings of sadness that at the time I chose to ignore with resignation that the future was out of my hands anyway. And so I go on, in a tangle of intuition, imagination, intellectualization, and emotion.

I sit here staring at a Christmas card my sister sent me and think about Kant's idea that the state of mind of the beholder influences what he perceives in life, and our minds not only conform to reality, but reality conforms to our minds. The card is a small black and white drawing by the Australian cartoonist, Luenig. A man is pulling a rickety homemade cart across a vast expanse of land which reminds me a lot of the Outback. In the cart are three small creatures. The sky is black except for a circle of light that surrounds the little travellers. As they move toward an endless horizon, their gaze is fixed upon a star that is hanging from a pole that has been rigged to the cart. They have smiles on their faces, which are radiant with hope and a sense of purpose.

Cherie Bremer-Kamp, a native of Queensland, Australia, is trained and educated as a nurse and mid-wife. She has lived and worked in Nepal, Holland, New Zealand and the United States. In 1978 she was a member of the American K2 expedition. In 1985 she and her husband, Chris Chandler attempted the north face of Kanchenjunga on which Dr. Chandler died and Cherie suffered severe frostbite resulting in the loss of her fingers and toes. Cherie currently lives in Sausalito, California with her two children Annapurna and Daniel. She recently published LIVING ON THE EDGE an account of her attempt of the world's third highest mountain the 28,168 foot Kanchenjunga.

Women On The Rocks, Way Back Then
Ruth Dyar Mendenhall

Because of the passage of time, I have advanced from climber to pioneer woman climber.

I started climbing rocks in Southern California in 1938. Alpine techniques had been introduced to both the Los Angeles and San Francisco areas in 1931 during Robert L. M. Underhill's visit from New England. A Rock Climbing Section (usually referred to as the RCS) was established in the mid-thirties in the Southern California (now Angeles) Chapter of the Sierra Club. At the time I took up the sport, the popularity of climbing was rapidly rising. Most of the pioneer rock climbers were men, but several outstanding women climbers had already retired from climbing or overlapped with me. Now that I am considered a Pioneer nearly fifty years later, modern women climbers have expressed an interest in the status of women climbers of that day. A question occasionally asked is whether we climbed with men or mostly with each other. The short simple answer to that is that we did not have enough climbers to sort them out by gender.

There were seldom more than three or four serious women climbers in Southern California at any one time, often only one or two compared to, perhaps, six to a couple of dozen men. Besides that, the boys and girls enjoyed climbing together. Most respected their own and each other's abilities and limitations. A few fellows, usually young gymnasts, seemed to feel diminished if a girl made a pitch they couldn't. But I remember very little machismo, or for that matter machisma, among us. Of course, a mixture of these attitudes did surface occasionally. For example, at a Tahquitz Rock climb, the man who was trip leader was arranging the ropes for the day's climbs. He asked me to lead a visitor from Switzerland up the Fingertip Traverse. Although I had made the climb, I was in my first season and somewhat lacking in confidence. I was on the verge of declining when another man nearby, who really had nothing to do with the matter, spoke to me: "Ruth! You shouldn't! You had only three or four hours of sleep last night." That decided me. I agreed to lead the rope, off-handedly collected my equipment and my second, and went. Years later I discovered by chance that I had acquired a modest fame in Europe as a rock climber.

Other women in our club had been making their mark in the climbing world: Mary Jane Edwards, Adrienne Applewhite (Jones), the first woman to climb the East Face of Mt. Whitney, LaVere Daniels (Aulie), who appeared in a professional movie short, "Three on a Rope," and was the first woman to climb Temple Crag, 12,999 feet. May Pridham, who had made assorted climbs with her sister and other girls before she ever heard of rope techniques, and who provided our newssheet with skiing and climbing cartoons so pertinent that they are famous in Sierra Club publications to this day. Elsie Strand and Agnes Fair. We didn't think of ourselves as women climbers, but as women who liked to climb. The field of mountaineering and rock climbing was wide open to all comers.

I had grown up having outdoor adventures with various of my three sisters and occasional cousins (our brother was too conservative). We had hiked, backpacked, camped, and gone on wilderness fishing trips. Though we had never heard of rock climbing, we had indulged in ascents of some of the basalt formations in Spokane, Washington. I later classified some of these climbs as fourth class; we should have been roped. Though all my sisters climbed to some extent in later years, I was the only one to develop such a passion for climbing that I pursued it for thirty-five seasons.

From Spokane, I had come to Southern California as a college graduate in need of a job, my school having assigned all its scarce job openings that year to men. A relative offered me secretarial work with one of the State Relief Organizations of the time. I was lonely, homesick, and displaced in both occupation and geography. When I discovered the Ski Mountaineers Section of the Sierra Club, my life improved immeasurably. When I found out that many of the skiers became rock climbers when the snow melted, I thought I had been catapulted into Eden. Don't laugh! After all, there allegedly was an apple tree in eden. And due to a childhood of tree climbing, I soon realized that apple trees are the horticultural equivalent of sound granite.

My situation was not unlike that of many young people of that time, the latter years of the Great Depression. Some were unemployed; many held poorly paying jobs and worked hard not to lose them. We hungered for fun, adventure, and companionship.

These were available in the skiing and climbing set--and at that time had the added advantage of not costing much.

In the late 1930's there were no ski lifts except for a few short rope tows. The Ski Mountaineers gave instruction. They also raised money and provided the manpower to build and maintain ski huts in nearby mountains. Hut fees were twenty-five cents a night. Entertainment, often complete with a member's accordion at the end of a steep trail, was free.

Rock climbing was even cheaper. Our club furnished most of the equipment. Ropes were 90-foot and 130-foot seven-sixteenth inch manila, the best yachting line available. We compensated for its lack of stretch by dynamic belays. Steel carabiners were imported from Germany. The same was true of soft iron pitons until the duty became so high that local manufacture was arranged. Quarter-inch manila was used for slings and prusiks. We sewed leather patches onto pants and shirts to protect us from the friction of body rappels. We wore old jeans and very jaunty, individual felt hats. Ice axes and piton hammers were personal equipment, and we often had only one to a rope. For footgear in the high mountains, we had men's work shoes or old leather ski boots nailed with tricounis. For rock climbing we wore tennis shoes or crepe-soled basketball shoes. With this gear, the better climbers of the time put up routes judged very difficult to this day, and others followed them. In recent years a male climber remarked in my hearing, "Imagine climbing the Mechanic's Route (at Tahquitz) in tennis shoes!" I said, "I don't have to imagine it. I did it."

In my first season, I attended RCS climbs almost every weekend. There were one-day or half-day instructional climbs locally, at Stony Point, Eagle Rock, and Devil's Gate Dam (until the authorities plastered it with concrete). Here anyone could learn elementary rope handling, belaying, and safety. Weekend climbs were held at Tahquitz Rock. This thousand-foot wedge of glorious granite rock, on the south side of Mt. San Jacinto above Idyiwild, seemed to offer endless possibilities for new routes. Only ten had been established by early 1938. And for three-day weekends, we went to the High Sierra, its stupendous East Face readily accessible from the south. Climber's vacations were usually spent in the Sierra. Foreign climbing, except for a rare venture to Canada, was at that time beyond the scope of our group.

Over the weekend of July 4, 1938, I had my first taste of scaling one of the fourteen-thousand-foot peaks in the Palisades, west of Big Pine in Owens Valley. The backpack was three or four miles of easy trail to Third Lake at about 10,000 feet. Parties attacked North Palisade (14,242 feet) and Mt. Sill (14,162 feet) by assorted routes. I was one of two ropes that made a new route up the North Buttress (now called the Swiss Arete in climbers' guides). We had two experienced rope leaders. The rest of us were all in our first season of climbing. The two men, whose bent was really not rock climbing, didn't seem to appreciate the exposure. I was so exhilarated by my first ascent of a real mountain, by the elevation and difficult moves, and by the lovely surroundings that, though I kept my cool, I was running over with sheer joy. We made the summit and descended by an easier way. For years afterwards, my rope leader twitted me about our return to camp. He claimed that, when our friends came into view beside their little campfires, I exclaimed, "Let's run, so they don't think we're tired."

Over Labor Day that year, eleven RCS members, nine men and two women, made the strenuous backpack, largely cross-country, over Pinnacle Pass to camp at East Face Lake at over 13,000 feet. Next day we all climbed 14,495-foot Mt. Whitney's East Face by the Sunshine-Peewee Route (now more decorously referred to as the East Buttress). The difficulty of the pack-in made a much more lasting impression on my mind than the climb itself.

Backpacking equipment of the day included Trapper Nelson packboards of wood and canvas, tortuous for neck and shoulders. Many of us had made our own sleeping bags. A pillow factory blew goose down into the tubes. Down cost $3 a pound, but as we often remarked, down was going up. A shelter was rarely needed, since it "never" rained in the Sierra until after nylon and plastic were invented. Our foods came from the grocery store in the form of cheese, sausage, spaghetti, cereals, dried fruits, crackers and candy. We didn't miss freeze-dried or "instant" foods since there weren't any. But we did have Primus stoves from Sweden.

On our trips the mountains rang all day, and sometimes far into the night, with puns, jokes, yodels, shouts, and laughter, and with the singing and pinging of pitons going deeper into the cracks with each whack of the hammer. It was a gay and happy period in our lives, certainly not carefree, but light-hearted and filled with good comradeship. Both men and women became close friends through their mountain activities and related pursuits.

We were often together evenings as well as weekends. We held meetings, gave parties, promoted "ski rallies" to raise funds for the ski huts, and published our Ski Mountaineers and Rock Climbing Sections' newssheet, The Mugelnoos. For many a year I was chief honcho for The Mugelnoos, named after what is now called a mogul and our Ski Mountaineers chairman George Bauwen's Austrian accent. I kept the newssheet crammed with puns (one issue claimed forty-nine puns), cartoons, and facts that made climbing history. The first ascent of the Eigerwand was noted in August, 1938. We also had a correspondent from Byrd's third Antarctic Expedition of 1939-40. The Expedition's official artist, Leland Curtis, was a member of the Ski Mountaineers Section.

Transportation to Section affairs posed the usual problems. Most of the men and a few women drove old cars, and the rest of us were courtesy or paying passengers. Some of the crowd still lived at home, a very few were married, others occupied rooms or apartments, alone or with friends. Gradually a few of us, whose situations and yearnings were similar, conceived the idea of starting a cooperative coeducational boarding house for climbers and skiers. We weren't quite ready for a serious romance, though that came along soon. We weren't into what are now called relationships. Our mutual and overwhelming desire was a place to live that would be spacious, enjoyable, and of necessity economical -- A HOME. The concept was rather far-out for the times. That it actually became a reality -- and a success -- seems a little surprising even now.

Ideas had been exchanged, and the prospective personnel reduced to six for a start: three men (Howard Koster, Glen Warner, and John Mendenhall) and three women (Olga Schomberg, my sister Joan Dyar (Clark), who had recently joined me in California, and I). We were between the ages of twenty-one and thirty. The men and I were dedicated climbers and also skied. Olga and Joan climbed a little and skied a lot. Our first practical need was to find the right house.

All the rental houses we had looked at up to late April 1939 were unsuitable--inconveniently located, too costly, too stark, too small. Then came an incredible stroke of luck. En route to a ski mountaineering venture on Mt. San Gorgonio, John and I took a look at a house for rent in northeastern Los Angeles. There it was! Big enough; on a streetcar line; cheap enough ($60 a month); and fully and nicely furnished, right down to table linens, a radio-phonograph, an encyclopedia, a piano, a fireplace and a mantel clock. On top of all that, the landlady, Grace Schults, had been a

Sierra Club member. She seemed to have neither questions nor qualms about our unconventional plans. We telephoned our prospective housemates to inspect the place and went off skiing. Early the next week, the chosen six assembled to look together at this gem of a house. The decision seemed so momentous that for a short time we even ran out of wisecracks. We voted *"yes."*

The rooms were apportioned among us without problems. Joan and I had the big upstairs bedroom and Olga the small one. John, who needed a little peace and quiet for his engineering studies, had the third. Howard and Glen took the big downstairs bedroom. Mr. and Mrs. Schults retained a small corner apartment. Their son occupied a little knotty-pine building at the back of the lot. That was Monday. The next Saturday, May 5, 1939, we moved in.

Six people arrived with their accumulated belongings. These turned the ample front porch into a sort of junkyard of hickory skis, bamboo ski poles, desks, boots, carpets, a drafting board, lamps, ropes, a typing chair, canned milk, and my typewriter. Before getting organized, we looked again at our brown stucco palace. Enthusiasm mounted. Glen and I were so pleased at the back lawn that we turned somersaults all over it. Roses, syringa, and apple blossoms were in bloom. Mrs. Schults, with what turned out to be typical kindness and thoughtfulness, had cooked us a big pot of split pea soup and disappeared into her own rooms. Pea soup became a symbolic delicacy that for many years was ceremoniously served at Base Camp anniversaries and reunions.

A few days later, as all gathered at our new home for dinner, we held a house meeting. Our residence had to have a name, of course. After contemplating the fact that we had all heard of Green Gables and Seven Gables, Howard suggested Composition Roof, and Joan came up with Clark Gables. Eventually we chose Base Camp. We decided to try out this system of housework: a girl and a fellow would buy food and cook dinner together for one week (breakfasts were individually prepared, and we were seldom home for lunches); a girl and a fellow would wash dinner dishes; and a girl and a fellow would do the cleaning, yard work, household laundry, and everything else. We would have the same partner for three weeks, then switch partners and start all over. This plan worked so well that we stuck to it with trade-offs and variations, for the duration.

None of us had ever been in charge of running a household, and we found the job novel and even hilarious. Before we moved in, our contemporaries told us it "wouldn't work." It did, and so did we. Of course we didn't have the same tastes and talents. Some were better cooks than others, Howard the best of us all. One of our male visitors did remark that he "just couldn't see why the men should be compelled to cook." It really took two to run the 1915 washing machine in our small back cellar. It had two large copper tubs, leaky hoses, an electric wringer, and frightening gears. We kept each other up to a high standard of living. I once overheard Olga reprimanding Glen for getting out a clean tablecloth. Glen replied firmly that he would rather eat off newspapers than use the dirty one.

Dinners were nutritious and tasty, though sometimes we were up till midnight the preceding evening preparing jello, shelling peas, and other tasks. Mother's Day came around soon after we were settled, so we planned a special dinner for the five available parents and grandmothers. Olga and I planned the menu: roast beef, gravy, new potatoes, asparagus, aspic salad, rolls, coffee, and strawberry pie. Much preparation had to be done the preceding afternoon, since most of us planned to attend a practice climb Sunday morning. It had been my custom to rush off to climbs at the earliest possible moment, and return as late as feasible, and the fellows were even more addicted to this procedure. That Sunday Glen left early to take the ropes, which were stored in our living room window seat, to Eagle Rock. But the rest of us were putting the finishing touches on the dinner preparations. I was baking pies and dusting, Joan fixing bouquets, Howard doing the wash, and John cleaning house and preening the parking strip. I put the roast in the oven and set the timer to turn it on at noon; those who stayed home watched breathlessly to be sure it did. Eventually John, Olga and I were off to the climb, where we were greeted by remarks about our lateness. I explained that we were too busy keeping house to climb, a shock to those who knew us.

When we returned to Base Camp, the roast was snapping away in the oven. John had set the table for eleven. Chairs, plates, and silverware were carefully arranged so the guests would have the best. Our invited guests duly arrived, and the affair went off smoothly. The older ladies seemed properly impressed. After their departure, we spent the rest of the evening praising ourselves, cleaning up, and hurling insults at each other.

During that summer, we entertained countless guests, some-times too many. We gave special dinners for aunts, cousins, old friends, and mostly our climbing and skiing friends. Drop-in guests sometimes seemed a bit startled by in-house arguments about who would stake them to the meal (twenty cents a head). Later we decided we should argue it out in private.

Since early 1938, I had been editing our newssheet and putting it out at my apartment, with a few assistants both regular and ad hoc. The first time The Mugelnoos was mimeographed and mailed at Base Camp, a gang of thirty friends turned up for the occasion, probably more from curiosity than volunteerism. During the week, I had collected and rewritten the news and cut the stencils, with John and Glen helping me. The mimeographing, an inky procedure, fitted ideally into the back porch. Our friends were perfect guests. They invited themselves, did most of the work, entertained themselves and their hosts, cleaned up the place, and went home. Mugelnoos-night parties became traditional, and Base Camp was turned into a social center as well as a source of information about almost anything. There was a lot of togetherness, but our rooms were strictly private territory.

Guests or not, there was always something going on at Base Camp. Joan on the piano and Howard on his tuba played duets. Some of us were always poring over mountaineering books such as Climbing Days by Dorothy Pilley and The Romance of Mountaineering by R. L. G. Irving. Four who were taking a first aid course had hysterics over prone-pressure artificial respiration. At dinners, the male cook was to sit in the armchair, which we called the Papa Chair; but if the male cook was absent, the female cook did the honors. There was a decided advantage to having two cooks--no matter what was fixed, there was always one other person to praise it.

We were heavy on economy, especially Howard, who occasionally overdid it. On one occasion he spied an uneaten cob of corn among the garbage, and indignantly bore it into the kitchen to add to the lima beans he was preparing. I intervened in sanitary horror. Howard was adamant. A wrestling match ensued, during which I succeeded in messing up the corn so even Howard admitted it was unfit to eat. Then we settled down to a laughing spree, and for several days our jokes seemed to center around garbage.

At dinner, humor seemed to be at its height. We often had jello for dessert, because it was cheap and easy to prepare. Its basic ingredients became a matter of speculation. Howard advanced a theory that it was made from horses' hooves. The encyclopedia revealed that gelatin was indeed extracted from animal tissues.

Horses were not specifically mentioned, but it was not uplifting to read of hides, glue, coated pills, and isinglass. When the first course was over, Glen leaned back in his purple shirt and said, "Well, bring on the isinglass." I glanced at the color of the dessert being served, and inquired if it was "strawberry roan." On another evening Joan had received a message to telephone a climber who was an intern. As she rose from the table, she remarked, "I have to call General Hospital." John inquired sternly, "Has your meal taken effect already?"

Sometimes we laughed so loudly that we would glance up and notice the next-door neighbor peering at us from her kitchen window and laughing right along with us. This neighbor was such an avid church-goer that we referred to her as the Christian Lady. We were somewhat surprised one day when she told Joan that we were "finer young people than some of the Christians she knew." Our landlady, Mrs. Schults, told us from time to time that we took better care of her property, and kept our house neater, than any tenant she ever had. Along with all this virtuosity, domesticity, and high jinx, we were living more economically than had seemed possible. About twenty dollars from each of us monthly covered all expenses, rent, food, telephone, newspaper and utilities.

We were usually gone weekends, climbing with each other and non-Base Camp friends. John D. Mendenhall had been attracted to the climbing scene since he was a child in Missouri. He is credited by Chris Jones in Climbing in North America with being the first known person "to consciously belay in the Sierra Nevada." He had figured it out from library books and practiced with like-minded friends. That summer John and I went on many private climbs together. Our main goal was to make pioneer ascents of the north side of Strawberry Peak in the local mountains. The cliff could be seen from the Angeles Crest Highway and was approached by a long hot trail and by way of a firebreak amid Southern California's chaparral. Our first route occupied us for several Sundays, and was so devious that we named it the Strawberry Roam.

Over the weekend of July 4, 1939, John and I planned to join the Rock Climbing Section's trip to the Minarets in the Sierra. We had spent our evenings the week before poring over maps and guidebooks. Our entire household was preparing for other trips. Ropes were inspected for flaws, crampons were tried on, boots waxed, pants patched. And our household duties were always with us.

John and I both had to work Saturday morning. After that nothing went quite right. Our transportation didn't leave till mid-afternoon. We reached the end of the road at midnight. John and I staggered out of our bags at 5 a.m. and backpacked seven miles to the RCS camp, easily identifiable because in those days our climbers rarely saw anyone else in the mountains. Due to inexperience and over-optimism, we thought we could make an afternoon climb of the Underhill-Eichorn Route on Banner Peak (12,957 feet). The approach seemed long, but we moved fast when we got on the rock. The difficulty increased as we climbed, and by 6 p.m. the summit was still far above us. We bivouacked. We always had extra food in the rucksack, but it was a cold cramped night on our ledge. We slept, we shivered, we nibbled on our Famine Ration of horrid drugstore bargain chocolate. We laughed: climbers always seemed to think the worse the conditions, the funnier. It was a new experience for me, and I thought that since I was there I should make the best of it. The cliffs dropped precipitously below, a star fell, the Banner Glacier gleamed in the moonlight. A red star rose over White Mountain Peak across Owens Valley. At around 4 a.m. the eastern sky was filling with an orange light. Before 5, pale sunlight lay across our ledge. We ate snow and our last lemon drops for breakfast and descended to camp. We were teased for years about this bivouac, as a couple of weeks later we announced our engagement.

When we told Howard about our plans, he exclaimed, "But you can't get married and move out of Base Camp." It turned out that we could and did. But Howard, true to his philosophy, in early 1941 brought his own bride to live at Base Camp for a few months, presumably under housekeeping tutelage of the residents.

By mid-August of 1939, the Romance in Mountaineering had struck again. Dick Jones and Adrienne Applewhite announced their engagement. Our household and its circle of friends rose to the occasion. On my birthday, August 16, a surprise party was arranged at Base Camp for the two recently engaged couples. My gift from John was an ice axe, the peak of my desires. He had die-stamped in the steel head the words "HAPPY BIRTHDAY 1939" on one side, and "RUTH FROM JOHN" on the other. After that presentation, Cupid came, in the flesh of a brawny mountain climber dressed in pink tights, a grass skirt, and wings, carrying a small bow and arrow. Gifts proliferated. The party ended with a turmoil of tissue paper, paper dishes, and cake crumbs in the living room. Glen said in his sage way, "Let's put the cake where the mice won't get it, and go to bed."

Despite mountain peaks and diamond rings, housework went on. Howard edged the front lawn, John mowed the back lawn, and I followed up with the sprinkler. I cooked a huge pot of stew that, with side dishes, kept dinners going for nearly a week. Green apples were falling from the tree that had been in bloom when we moved in. We picked them up for sauce and pies. Times were changing. Dick and Adrienne went on a Mass Honeymoon with a group of friends. Over Labor Day they bivouacked while down-climbing the East Face of Mt. Whitney. On the same weekend, John and I put up a new route on the East Buttress of Third Needle south of Whitney. The next Mugelnoos commented that our two-man rope was soon to be spliced. I quit my job: hereafter we would divide work differently. In the midst of a terrible 109 degree hot spell, we were married at the home of John's parents in the San Fernando Valley and left Base Camp for our own home. Two girls and a man replaced us. The Schults family moved out to make room for more new residents.

The institution of Base Camp as a residence and social head-quarters for skiers and climbers continued for over two more years. Sixteen different young people lived there, the maximum at any one time being ten, and the minimum six. This number included nine women and seven men. Base Camp was reluctantly disbanded in October 1941 because of the difficulties of keeping up the number of residents; defense work and the draft, higher education and romance were taking their toll. John and I, on the brink of leaving the Los Angeles area for war work on the East Coast and elsewhere, put up a new route on Mt. Whitney, the Southeast Face. World War II scattered our crowd all over the world and changed our lives. But when we returned four years later, the mountains were waiting.

Wartime research had made great changes in mountaineering equipment and techniques, as well as in other things. Both men and women found changes in many aspects of life. And in another fifty years, women climbers of 1988, now Pioneer Women Climbers themselves, will find out how they fit into the climbing world of 2038.

Ruth Dyar with John Mendenhall, July 1939.

Ruth Dyar Mendenhall began climbing in 1938 and continued for thirty-five seasons. In those thirty five years she was responsible for routes all over the world.

Ruth was a member of the American Alpine Club and served on its board of directors and, for years, edited American Alpine News. Ruth wrote books and articles on climbing for beginners, about backpacking and outdoor cookery.

Ruth died in Seattle, Washington, in the Spring of 1989.

Climbing And The Art Of Peeing
Dorcas S. Miller

I was working as a river guide on the Penobscot and Kennebec rivers in Maine. My butt was wet so much that I got diaper rash, so on my days off I headed for the mountains. One of my co-workers was married to a ranger at Baxter State Park and I often visited Jean and John at their cabin at Chimney Pond, on the flank of Katahdin.

I'm not sure why I was looking for a challenge that summer. The Penobscot had a stretch of Class 5 water that was reputed to be the hardest commercially run white water on the east coast. That should have used up my adrenalin for the year. But I had pleasant (and, truth to tell, some not so pleasant) memories of rock climbing when I worked for Outward Bound in the early 1970s, and something about climbing attracted me that summer. One day in early September I hiked into Chimney Pond and asked the other ranger, who was a climber, if he would be interested in going out with me.

"Sure," Ben said, his face brightening. "I have tomorrow off. We could go over into the North Basin and climb Hanta Yo. Do you have shoes?"

"Oh, yes," I assured him. I'd brought along my climbing shoes: medium-weight Fabiano klettershoes. Ben was kind enough not to point out that they were classics.

The next morning we hiked into the North Basin. Autumn had arrived at this mountain of early winters. The mountain ash, birch, and blueberry had turned brilliant colors. The mountain cranberry and bearberry were heavy with fruit. Sun poured into the cirque and we basked in the warmth of an Indian summer day.

Hanta Yo is an eight-pitch climb that follows a long corner system to the right edge of the thousand-foot North Basin Wall. If Hanta Yo were in Yosemite or in Cannon, it would be a favorite beginner/intermediate climb. Tucked away in the North Basin, a six-hour drive and two-hour hike from Boston, the climb sees little activity. That day, Ben and I did the third or fourth ascent.

Ben fitted me out in a Whillans harness, which I had never worn before, and showed me how to remove protection. My climbing before that day had been limited to top-roping; climbing in most outdoor programs is used as a challenge rather than as a skills development activity.

We started up the wall, alone in that golden universe. The higher we got, the more world lay at our feet. Red and yellow mountains and dazzling lakes stretched beyond the lip of the basin.

About half way up, we had a bite to eat. I was so excited that I'd forgotten my lunch, so I shared Ben's gorp and water. I began thinking how nice it would be to take a leak, but I was much too shy to ask how to go about doing it. Clearly, I couldn't take off the Whillans--I wasn't sure I could get it buckled up right--and I didn't know how to rig up an alternate harness. I decided to wait until he was at the next belay, scrunch my shorts to one side, and pee down the pantleg. The system had worked well enough with a one-piece bathing suit when I was guiding.

It didn't work at all. I peed in my pants.

I turned my butt to the sun and hung out to dry when I was alone and backed into the rock when we shared the belay. At the top, Ben suggested changing to long pants because we had to bushwack to the trail. I enthusiastically agreed.

Hanta Yo was so exhilarating that we went out the next day and climbed Pamola Four, a ridge in the South Basin. Pamola Four is mostly fourth class, but we roped up because I was feeling the exposure and the stiff wind. That day, I asked how one could take a leak. Ben showed me how to use a chest harness: he became fascinated with the activity on Baxter Peak while I peed (this time not in my pants). Still it was all too cumbersome. I wanted an easy way.

We climbed at Acadia and then again at the Gunks. By this time, it was clear to both of us that we were interested in more than climbing together.

Ben loaned me a book, *Learning to Rock Climb* by Michael Loughman. It had lots of helpful tips for getting started, but the best part was the photographs of Amy Loughman. It was inspiring to see a woman about my size doing graceful, balanced moves on rock. In the dozen years I'd been guiding and teaching, there had been few women role models. I'd missed them.

As he gave me the book, Ben commented, "It's hard for people to climb together and be romantically involved. Issues in the relationship tend to interfere with climbing well together. I know several climbing couples who have gotten divorced. Loughman advises against climbing with your girlfriend, boyfriend, or spouse because it can strain the relationship. He ought to know. He and Amy are divorced."

Wonderful, I thought. I'm having a great time climbing and I'm excited about this new relationship, but chances are that I'll have to give up one or the other.

I'd been noticing that no one else was wearing klettershoes. In fact, on our last day at the Gunks, I overheard someone say, "Look at the funny shoes that girl has." I wanted to tell him that I'd been climbing in these funny shoes when he was in grade school, and that climbers had done first ascents of many of the climbs at the Gunks wearing these funny shoes. Have the weeners no sense of history? Besides, I'd whipped up Easy Overhang in my outdated shoes, while the fellow ahead of me whined and trembled and sweated in his E.B.s. State-of-the-art shoes aren't everything.

But they are something. If I wanted to improve, I should get a new pair of shoes. Ben suggested that we stop at Rock and Snow in New Paltz.

"OK, but you have to stay in the car," I said. I was extremely sensitive about being a woman in a world populated by men. So far, I'd seen one female climber--or rather, I'd seen her brand new E.B.s flapping in the breeze as she put both knees on a ledge. I did not want to be a "girlfriend," someone who knew nothing about the sport, someone who got dragged up routes her partner wanted to climb. I was fiercely independent and staked out my territory.

I wanted to go into the store, ask a lot of questions, and make my own decision. So I went into the store, asked a lot of questions, and decided I couldn't afford any of the shoes on the shelf. I also found out that Ben, who memorizes every equipment catalog and who used to work at REI, knew more about shoes than the salesman.

(Several months later, Ben's previous girlfriend returned a pair of P.A.s and a Whillans harness. Not a bad deal for me; she was my size.) It was November and the climbing season in New England was drawing to a close. "If you love climbing so much, don't you get frustrated when winter rolls around?" I asked Ben.

"Oh, it'll be ice climbing season soon," he said. "Want to come?"

"Forget it," I answered. "Too cold."

It was too cold, but I went anyway. I borrowed a pair of ancient hinged crampons with extra-long front points (which held me out from the ice) and put them on my three-quarter shank hiking boots (so the whole thing was pretty flexible) and used an old ice ax (which weighed twice as much as a new one). Since I'd never climbed ice before, I thought everything was just fine, except that I lost sensation in my feet and hands every time I went out.

"More clothes," Ben said.

I layered on poly, pile, wool, and nylon until I looked like the Pillsbury dough boy. I still didn't stay warm, but the excitement and challenge of this new activity balanced the excruciating pain of warming numb appendages--at least for the first two years. Then I began serious complaining.

Ben didn't understand. He thought I was kidding. Once, on a spring climb, my hands went dead; Ben was stripped down to a single layer and was still sweating. It wasn't just the wrist loops or the fact that I was gripping the handles tightly. My hands could go numb anywhere, any time. We started doing comparison testing and sure enough, my hands were always colder. Feet and nose, too, though the nose wasn't as crucial to climbing.

My experience rock climbing and ice climbing have shown me that Ben and I are so different that I really can't take many cues from him. Ben has a wide range of comfort; I get hot and cold easily and am constantly taking off and putting on clothing. He's six feet and four inches, while I'm five feet and five inches, so I have to make two delicate moves to get to the bucket he reaches easily. Ben is strong and I'm not; I have to move quickly and smoothly so I don't drain my strength. And, of course, he can pee even in all those winter clothes and a harness, while I have to disrobe and bare my butt to the elements.

I couldn't change my anatomy but I could, perhaps, change my clothing. For the first two winters we climbed together, I used a swami, but I wasn't satisfied. It was too loose or too tight, the holsters slid around and sagged, and I always felt like a klutz. Although I could take a leak, it was still an act of bravery. I liked my Whillans, but there was the perennial problem: peeing.

I'd read an article by a woman in Alaska who had put zippers in her pants. I hauled out my sewing machine and experimented, putting a coil zipper along the crotch seam of my poly underwear (with the zipper on the outside), wool pants, and wind pants. Lo and behold, I could take a leak without removing my harness or pulling down my pants. I had to get used to peeing through my pants--at first I felt like I was going to pee in them--but after a time it felt pretty normal. Solving that problem actually improved my ability to deal with the cold, since I'd been drinking too little water and getting dehydrated, which made me even colder.

I also got better clothes and equipment. Plastic boots, for instance, are the ticket for toasty toes: I can cinch down on the crampon straps and not cut off the circulation. But I still haven't entirely resolved the cold problem. My Baltimore-born body simply doesn't deal well with the stop-and-start rhythm of ice climbing. Skiing and snowshoeing make more sense because I have more control over the pace of the activity.

(I solved the rock climbing dilemma, not with zippers but with elastic-waisted clothing. I found I could pull down shorts, sweats, or lycra, pee, and wiggle them back up under the harness. This maneuver is very difficult with zippers or buttons.)

My approach to peeing is like my approach to climbing. I can't do things the way that other people do them because the other people are usually taller, stronger, and male. Although I watch other people climb and pay attention to how they use their feet, how they balance off one smear to reach another, and how they lean off a bucket, I have to translate all that into my framework. I hate it when someone tries to tell me what to do; that person usually doesn't understand my reach and balance. On the other hand, if I see a person my size--usually that's a woman--do a hard climb, I'm more inclined to take a crack at it because there's a fairly direct translation from her to me. One spring I saw a woman leading Deception Crack at Stone Mountain and I thought, "I could do that." I later led it; it was my first 5.9.

For a long time, I wasn't interested in leading. The process of placing protection seemed to come between me and the rock. During my previous life, when I top-roped, it was just me and the rock. All the new gizmos inhibited my climbing.

Besides, I was always climbing at my limit when I followed Ben. The idea of leading those same climbs was terrifying. No thanks, I said to Ben's frequent encouragement to lead.

Two things changed my mind. I went to see Rosie Andrews and her slide show, "Women climbers in the 80's." I was inspired by her observations and slides of women climbers. After the show, someone asked her about starting to lead. "Choose something you've done a dozen times before, something on which you feel really comfortable," she said. It made perfect sense. If I tried leading something easy, then I'd learn about placing pro and build up my confidence.

She said something else that struck home. "Women are most limited by their attitudes. We're not brought up to be aggressive. Most women are not willing to risk falls. To be really good, you have to take some falls." That made sense, too, but I wasn't as sure I'd take that advice. I wasn't sure how good I wanted to be.

The second event was that Ben and I went to Stone Mountain, North Carolina, and I fell in love with friction. We had been doing mostly cracks: cracks at Katahdin, Acadia, Cathedral, and the Gunks. But we'd done very little friction.

I felt free on friction. On the easier climbs, I felt like I was walking, not climbing. Placing pro didn't get between me and the rock because there was little pro to place--many of the climbs at Stone Mountain are bolt-protected. Leading at Stone Mountain and later at Whitehorse Ledge bolstered my confidence on other kinds of rock, too.

Because I know few women climbers, I've enjoyed reading books and articles. I also pay attention to what sociologists would call the oral tradition. Ben has a stack of stories gleaned from years of reading climbing magazines.

He told me about Diana Hunter, who led a new climb when her partner--Henry Barber--backed off. I thought about her the day I led the Byzantine at Acadia. Neither Ben nor Dan could get started and I wanted to give it a try. Dan insisted I take the rack. I'd done almost no leads, so I said it was silly to take it along. I waltzed by the crux. When I got to a rest, Ben told me to put in the #6 hex. "What's that?" I answered.

I thought about Miriam Underhill one night when I helped on a rescue in Huntington Ravine. I'd just read the chapter in *Give Me the Hills* in which she describes an early trip to Tuckerman's Ravine on Mt. Washington. She and friends had spent a full day skiing and were so whipped they couldn't possibly take another step. Two of their party didn't return that evening; however, and she embarked on a rescue.

Ben and I had gotten up at 4:30 a.m. and hiked in to Huntington to do Pinnacle Gully, my first alpine ice climb. We did the route and then hiked back down to the car, arriving at sunset. There, we heard about an accident in the ravine and volunteered to help, as we are both emergency medical technicians. Secretly, I hoped I wouldn't be needed, but the director said he could use anyone who knew how to walk with crampons. Even I qualified.

The rescue went smoothly. I took my turn helping to pull the banana-boat sled. It was a quiet, still night on Mt. Washington.

The clear sky shone with a million stars. I was the only woman there and I felt protective of the fellow in the sled who didn't even have a girlfriend to call from the hospital. We finished at midnight and got home at 3 a.m. I had relived Miriam's story, with my own cast of characters.

It would be a great end to this story if I could write, "My climbing blossomed and I became an extremely bold and talented climber. I did a first ascent of a 1,000-foot wall in the northern Rockies and led all of the hard pitches, and I was asked to join a 1995 Himalayan climbing expedition." Then I could describe how climbing has changed my life and opened new worlds to me.

But I haven't become an extremely bold and talented climber. I'm an intermediate, recreational climber who doesn't even aspire to do the desperates. I've dealt with some small challenges (like how to leak on a belay) and some big challenges (like how to be both a climbing partner and a spouse--Ben and I have managed to survive the odds). In between, I've climbed a lot of rock and had fun doing it.

Dorcas S. Miller, a former Outward Bound instructor and river guide, helped found and was a member of the board of directors of Women Outdoors, Inc., a national program that provides women an opportunity to develop outdoor and leadership skills. She has written for Canoe, Climbing, and Sea Kayaker magazines and published five books: The Healthy Trail Food Book; The Maine Coast: A Nature Lover's Guide; Track Finder; Berry Finder; and Winter Weed Finder. She is currently a free-lance writer and editor.

Dorcas Miller on
Spring Fever, Parks
Pond Bluff, Maine.
Photo by
Jerry Cinnamon

Alison Osius.
Photo by
Brian Bailey

The Naked Edge
Alison Osius

Muttering in exasperation, Coral Bowman set up a rappel. She and Sue Giller were a couple hundred feet up a climb they'd been planning to do all summer, and the thin nine-millimeter rope they were using to haul a day pack had snagged. Coral planned to rappel down her 11-millimeter climbing rope, free the other, and ascend again with Sue reeling in the 11-mil from above. She leaned back--and then she was falling through the air. The 11-mil had unclipped from the carabiner she'd attached it to. Sue's eyes met Coral's for an instant, saw surprise and disbelief. She's dead, Sue thought. I'm dead, Cora thought.

Just then Coral stretched out her arms, clutched, and caught the skinny haul rope in her hands. As she tried to hang on, Sue saw no slowdown. Coral slid and slid, burning trenches into her palms. Then her speed began to decrease. Fifty feet down, she stopped. Before her hands stiffened into useless hooks, she swung to a ledge, and clipped into some slings that were there.

Coral's was a supernatural feat--like a mother lifting a car off her child. Sue rappelled down, and pitch by pitch, lowered her friend to the ground. "I almost died!" Coral said when Sue first reached her, but neither said it again.

When Coral, possibly then the best woman climber in the world, and Sue had started on The Naked Edge in Colorado, they hoped to become the first female team up a route the climbing community virtually exalted. That was in 1979, six years after Jim Erickson and Duncan Ferguson first free climbed (ascended without using mechanical aids) The Edge. Their ascent of what had once been an unthinkable line opened up a new realm in climbing in the 1970s, a golden era of hard first ascents.

The Edge, which begins several hundred feet off the ground and ends 750 feet up, saw little traffic that decade. If you'd done it, you'd arrived in the climbing world.

I first heard of The Edge the year after Erickson and Ferguson's feat. It was my first real season of rock climbing and I was in North Wales, teaching at the Plas y Brenin mountaineering center, and so I was virtually an alien to American climbing.

But there was one route whose name I, like other foreign climbers, knew. More than the Nose Route of El Capitan, more than Astroman in Yosemite, we knew The Naked Edge. The name, and the shape, captivated us. The Edge flew upward in a rising prow, sailed and lifted above the world, above ordinary, earthly things.

And it was the film. That's where I, transfixed, first saw the Naked Edge. "Break On Through" was very dramatic, if overly body-beautiful as far as the luxurious flexing of the principals went. The film captured the dizzying height and steepness, the exotic raw presence of The Edge.

I sat next to my friend Charlie, who'd seen the film before; at one point he warned in a whisper, "This part's horrific." The lead climber, noisy and panting, wildly stuffed his fists into the final crack, which leaned out over bottomless air. Here, the film went a lurid, filtered red--well, maybe green, but my memory thinks red--just in time to show him arcing into midair. I felt a sick gladness that it was him out there and not me. The film showed the guy falling again and again, bouncing on his rope each time.

I remember with acute clarity my awestruck and sinking realization: I will never be able to climb that. There are some things in life I know and accept I can never do. I will never be able to climb that.

It was 1980, and I was 21, just out of college and used to the optimistic idea of physical things as possibilities. But not this thing.

I had learned to climb during spring of my freshman year at Middlebury College in Vermont. But the only steady, rather than scattered, climbing I had done was during a junior year in Scotland. After graduation, when I went to Wales, I told myself, I'll just have this one full season of climbing before I look for a real job on a newspaper. On the rock climbing scale, whose technical difficulty then went from 5.0 to 5.12 (according to a route's steepness and the size of its holds, not its length) I hoped to "get solid leading 5.9." Three of the Naked Edge's five pitches (150-foot ropelengths) were 5.11. That meant their grade was just below the scale's ceiling (only a few American climbers could climb 5.12 then). As my friend Becky termed the grade 5.11, "That's you and God."

That summer in Wales I climbed almost every day, and was ever more intrigued by the sport's movements and situations. And while one reason for the headiness was that things unexpectedly became possible--my leading went a grade farther than I'd thought it could--I never dared think about The Edge.

Before that season ended, I'd decided I'd take just one more summer to climb, got a job instructing in southern California, and paid a visit to that climbers' mecca, Yosemite. There I heard (incorrect) talk that Coral's rope had been covered with blood from her hands. Neil, a climber who had to leave Yosemite for back-East obligations, mentioned that he was going by way of Colorado. "There's a climb I want to do there," he said.

"The Edge," someone instantly concluded, correctly.

A week or two later, Neil wrote me a long, thrilled letter; he obviously wanted to record the experience. His childish exclamations were meant to be funny, but his exuberance rang true. "The Naked Edge! That's THE EDGE, reindeer! It's the neatest, coolest, greatest climb ever!"

I also remember that a month or two later when another climber, coolly asking about Neil and assessing him as up-and-coming, said "Neil's done The Edge, right?"

"Right," I said.

"He take any falls?" Only two, I replied, on the fourth pitch, on the overhang above the chimney, because he didn't know which way to go. The questioner nodded sagely, though like me he'd never done the route. We knew about it play-by-play.

By winter I figured I'd need just one more summer to climb, and so warm weather '82 found me instructing in Washington State. That fall, I joined a women's climbing exchange to France. Sue Giller was one of our group of five.

She told me the Edge story. I asked about why Coral had quit climbing after that day, and Sue said she had called the experience a "wake-up call" and that it had made her question her reasons for climbing. For Sue, the experience was a watershed. As an extremely conservative climber, she had felt herself immune to such accidents. After that incident--which would have not happened had Coral backed-up her rappel carabiner with another--Sue decided to be as safe as humanly possible about things she could control, and to simply accept those things she couldn't. She went on to climb extensively in the Himalayas.

By that time I'd also heard about Jimmy Collins, who had a fight with his girlfriend and then soloed--climbed without a rope--the Naked Edge. The previous five times he'd done the route, he'd always fallen on the fifth pitch.

I spent the next three of my "just one more" climbing summers in New Hampshire, also teaching climbing. One June, driving through Colorado after a winter newspaper job in Salt Lake City, I stopped and visited Sue in Boulder. I saw the Naked Edge for the first time, and actually felt a pang of disappointment--it wasn't as big as I'd imagined.

I went climbing with an old college friend, Dave, who lived in Boulder. Surprisingly, he hadn't yet done the Edge, and we talked of that as an option. By now I had climbed enough at its grade to know, rationally, I should do OK on it. But I was oddly, furtively glad when it rained the next two days, and then I had to leave. I had a sense of wanting to be really ready for the route, of wanting to climb in the area more first. Stronger yet, I suspect, was this: if you don't try, you can't fail. Or thrash.

A year ago this month I went back to Boulder. And one of the hot, sunny days that otherwise blend hazily in my mind was Edge Day, partly made such because for once no one else was on the route. Over the years, as the number and skills of climbers increased, the climb became well-travelled. It was on many a climber's Hit List.

Actually, this didn't start out to be the big day. Neil and I arrived at the cliffs late, having first done a long errand. In the parking lot we found our friend Dan, "burned out" on climbing after several weeks at it. He was annoyed that we were late. I countered that the last he'd said the night before was that he probably wouldn't join us. He disagreed.

Along came blond Brooks, whom I didn't know well. Plans of action batted back and forth, and The Edge was one. But Neil had blitzed up the thing again only the week before, Dan also had done it twice, and Brooks had tried once, and doubted he was fit enough to fare better.

Last summer, Dan had raved about The Edge. It had been the goal of his whole season, he and his partner had diligently trained for it; when the time came, they met with perfect weather and no other parties. Psyched up, concentrating fabulously, each climbed better than he ever had. "We transcended ourselves," Dan later said with surprise.

Today, my three cohorts said they'd come along, but didn't want to do any leading. (The leader inserts metal wedges called "protection" into cracks in the wall; if he falls, the rope catches on the last one he placed. At the end of each pitch, he pulls in the rope for his partner, who risks no sizeable fall.) I was getting irritated. A big group of four would be slower than two pairs.

"You've never done it," Neil pointed out. "You should lead every pitch." What he also meant was, "You should want to." But Edge intimidation had intruded. Leading every pitch on a climb means you carry the whole ascent's momentum. "Well, how about swinging (alternating leads) a couple of times?" I said, and it was agreed.

We all started hiking to the base of the Redgarden Wall, whose upper reaches are The Edge. It was understood that, leaving the parking lot at about 3:00 and travelling so heavy, we'd have to motor. We hurried up three moderate pitches on another climb that led to The Edge's start, and then we were there. I stood at the base, putting together my rack (collection of protection) for the first lead, placing the pieces smallest-to-largest on their shoulder sling. I felt as I did the first time I had submerged with a scuba tank: Hold on, let me think about this a minute. But as I had then, I simultaneously moved along. I pulled into the first open-book corner and stood on a ledge, arranging my protection in the crack, and my plan for where feet and fingers would go. Plotting the moves is one of the biggest joys of climbing. Then it was time to roll, to force the final act of carrying out the strategy. I pulled on finger locks, walked my feet up on holds I seemed to see with great clarity, reached and made myself crank on a shallow finger slot, and then, just when I started shaking, I was at the top ledge. Done, surveying the first hurdle, I was exhilarated--the realization of where I was sunk in.

I pulled in rope as Dan moved up, extracting the hardware piece by piece, to join me at the stance. Ropework would be complicated among four, but someone decided that Neil would now lead on by to the next belay. He came efficiently along and joined us. Pleased to have done a workmanlike job, I thought he'd toss out the customary, "Nice lead," or some pleasantry.

He just said, "Why didn't you rack up?"

I hadn't put the hardware back into order. Neil pulled the gear sling off me, impatiently snapped and unsnapped carabiners, and pushed past. I hesitated, then said to Dan with a little laugh, "Thought he'd have said something more."

"We should have racked up," Dan said shortly.

We raced up two more pitches, finding steep but manageable rock. Somewhere in there Brooks must have offered to lead the fourth, the chimney pitch.

The experience felt like New Year's Eve. I used to think New Year's was supposed to be a really, really great time. But the fun usually felt forced. New Years' weren't the wild times I was supposed to have, and I ended up thinking I must be socially lame.

So it was now. I plastered smiles on my face, which must have been unsettling for everybody else, who didn't think to affect geniality. Then I shrugged and just joined into the hustling, terse mode of our ascent.

In fading light, I was going last up the bell-shaped chimney when I got stuck. Butt and back against one wall, feet and hands against the rock in front of me, I wasn't close to falling, it was just that somebody put the brakes on me. Go, go, I thought...then: I would, but I can't figure out how. After long minutes during which everyone must have wanted to shoot me, I moved rightwards on pinch holds, then up the overhang, forearms beginning to flame. Go right here or straight up? I wondered. Even as my eyes flickered back and forth, "Go right!" the peanut gallery shouted.

I had been slated to lead the fierce final pitch, but now the light was really draining. I'm a slow-to-middling climber; Neil is very fast, he knew the terrain, and when he asked if I wanted him to lead it, I said a relieved, disappointed yes. I tied in to the belay that Erickson had described as "a sloping doormat, suspended in space," surrounded by overhanging rock. Neil moved 10 feet up, then with a quick, deliberate jerkiness, around a corner. When my turn came, I had no time to plan. I bolted up to the smooth and awkward bulging corner, slick from many hands, and with luck hit a sequence that worked. To my vexation, Neil hauled on the rope from way above to speed things, and the tension pulled one piece of protection sideways so that I couldn't remove it. As I bellowed for slack, I wondered how Jimmy Collins had felt here looking between his legs at acres of air.

Dan, thinking I wanted to back down and re-plan a move, snapped, "No, just do it!" I had no breath to explain, but I thought, "Fuck you, you've already done it."

I moved up to the final crack, where Erickson, at the end of his strength, made a "lunge forever" that prevented a long fall. Hurry, I reminded myself. Panting, I karate-chopped my hands to the top of the crack, then clambered up as the angle slackened to horizontal. I was at the very top of The Naked Edge. I sat down. I said nothing.

At the Shawangunks cliffs in New York the locals have a name for a day of blasting up a number of very hard climbs they've got wired, even doing repeated laps on some. They call it a Rape Day. The first time I heard that term I recoiled. But the phrase was used in innocent tones, had become generic, part of the extensive 'Gunks slang. Eventually, I actually stopped noticing it. That night on The Edge, I thought of this term that I'd never used. And I thought, what a Rape Day. This ascent was demeaning to the route and all around.

Dan followed, then Brooks. And Brooks, who'd been so quiet all day, whooped. Bless his heart.

I told myself, well now, be real;. The rock doesn't care how you climb it. We just did The Edge! I joined him in shouting. I also thought about how it was actually pretty nice of Neil and Dan to retread a route they'd just repeated.

Then we all stumbled, crawled, and clambered down in the dark to the canyon floor.

Today, I work as a magazine editor. I can't climb every day any more, but I often boulder in the evenings and climb on weekends and vacations. A poster of the Naked Edge hangs above my desk, a powerful black-and-white showing two climbers, the rock kicking out above them, ropes whipping sideways in the wind, and birds swooping beneath. Recently, the climb came back to me. A writer had put together a nice slice-of-history piece on Jimmy Collins' free solo of The Edge. Editing it, I read of how Collins, then 20, did not consciously plan to do the solo that day. He did, however, head up a route that led to its start. At The Edge's base, he moved abruptly on to it. Then he just switched into auto pilot.

Only on the fourth pitch, when Collins had to commit to the intricacies of the chimney and overhang, did he finally admit to himself what he was doing. On the fifth, he took four deep breaths, then, not allowing himself to hesitate, cruised the bulge that had pushed him off so often.

I still had questions. So, glad but nervous to be contacting this legendary person, I phoned Jim to ask about just how the solo related to the famed argument. And why he'd since stopped climbing.The voice that answered the phone was friendly, animated, pleased to be talking about that long-ago day. Jim said that, contrary to rumor, he hadn't previously fallen off the last pitch every other time he had done the Edge. Just...four out of five. And it wasn't exactly his girlfriend with whom he'd had the argument...it was his ex-girlfriend.

One reason the pair had split, Jim said, was climbing's priority. He claimed that his solo act was not revengeful--not she'll be sorry--but an affirmation. "It was, 'This is what I do,'" he explained. Climbing was all he cared about, and he decided he could accept anything as long as it happened doing that.

"Why did you quit?" I asked. Jim said slowly that after a while he no longer wanted to put out the high intensity that climbing at the highest levels takes. And he decided that if he wasn't to climb at the top level, he didn't want to climb.

We chatted, and I said I'd done The Edge the summer before. Most of my friends would show faint or polite interest over that, but Jim exclaimed, "You did? Congratulations!" Pleasure stirred in me, but so did a rueful sense of anachronism. Yes, once people must have congratulated each other over it.

I laughed. "Well, it's kind of a sad story," I said. I explained the build-up, then the action as anticlimax, and tried to make it funny. Jim didn't really respond. I sensed he didn't understand or want to absorb my disappointment.

So I threw in what seemed like a chestnut about how happy I was at the top. He asked kind of wistfully, "So is it still a big deal for people to do it?" I hesitated, then said, "Yes."

Alison Osius attended Middlebury College and in 1984 received a Masters degree from Columbia University in journalism. Alison has written for a number of newspapers and magazines. One of the finest female rock climbers in the United States, Alison has climbed the Nose on El Capitan in Yosemite, Labyrinth Wall in New Hampshire, The Naked Edge in Colorado. Alison has also worked as a climbing guide in the eastern U.S. and in Wales and as a climbing instructor in California, Washington State and New Hampshire. Alison is a member of the American Alpine Club.

Alison is currently working on a chapter for THE COST OF ADVENTURE, an anthology dealing with dramatic mountain rescues and is a senior editor at Climbing Magazine.

Can This Trip Be Saved?
Wendy Roberts

Beyond the edges of Seattle stretches a vast wilderness where Espresso drinks cannot be found. I savored the totally beige foam in the bottom of my cup and consoled myself that this weekend's climbing at Squamish would really work out O.K. After all, we had all made a commitment to really TALK about our differences, and women are great at making commitments, right?

Jean and Margaret were already arguing over who had gotten the #2 Friend permanently stuck on their last Joshua Tree trip. Alison and Harriet were becoming increasingly frustrated as they tried to sort out what they were going to climb. Harriet wanted to work on learning to lead, preferably in the 5.5 to 5.6 range and mostly on cracks. Alison wanted to climb face, 5.9 to 5.10d, but she didn't feel like leading anything until she had warmed up on a few harder pitches.

My own climbing partner, Lana, was crashed out in the back of the van after having eaten an entire box of stale cheerios. She kept moaning something about needing to lose weight in order to "climb the hard stuff;" but we all gathered that her fast was not going well.

"Can this trip be saved?" I muttered to myself, sipping on the penultimate latte of the week.

It was high summer as Jana and I stared up at the too long ridge of Black Peak. My usual sandbag informant had assured me this route was only eight pitches. I hadn't led rock all year, but if we switched off it would only be four leads. No need to get gripped, just yet.

Eight pitches later we weren't even half-way up the ridge and I had a rather sinking feeling about the day. Sinking like the sun actually. I peered over my boots, down the fractured rock, and watched as the party of three guys behind us finished backing off to the glacier below.

Jana glanced up at the rest of the still very long-looking ridge and inquired, "Hey Wendy, would you feel OK if I said I didn't want to do any more leading?"

Hands shaking like aspen leaves in the up-coming autumn, I replied, "Oh, no problem, Jana. I think I can handle it."

Can this trip be saved?

Sure it could be saved; with only 11 more pitches, a midnight black hike out, and a couple of 1 AM phone calls back home. My partner back home had been eating chocolate and having diarrhea while contemplating calling mountain rescue.

Staggering into the 'North Winter' the day after Black Peak, I ran into Sharon, one of my least favorite female climbers. She is well known for telling women who came into the store asking about Women Climber's Northwest, that she didn't know if such a group existed. Sharon had of course been on our mailing list for two years before she scored a boyfriend to lead her up the hard stuff.

Responding to her question of what I'd been up to, I said, "Just got back from Black Peak at three o'clock this morning. Thought it was eight moderate fifth class pitches and ended up doing more than twice that many. But it was a beautiful day to be a slow party in the cascades."

"Yeah. I know, I was out too. We did a second ascent of Balanced Rock. It was about ten pitches. You know 5.9 to 5.11. Beautiful route, not too hard."

Can this climber be saved?! The last I heard she didn't lead rock at all because she "just liked following so much." So much for the concept that all female climbers are also feminists.

Back in the van, Harriet had indelicately pointed out that Alison only led 5.10 when clipping into bolts, and since she didn't know how to place pro, maybe she too could stand to lead a few 5.6's. Alison ignored Harriet's presence and amused us all by reading aloud the newspaper's latest work on the PTL Club scandal. (What does PTL stand for anyway...Pay The Lady?)

Speaking of sole saving, I remembered my expletives as I had once again contemplated a Devil's club thicket from the inside out. It all began innocently enough as I staggered off the plane from Japan, having just spent 70 days at sea on a Japanese research vessel. The 14 hour workdays, and all the chundering you could handle in between, had left me pretty trashed. It was Friday night of Labor Day weekend. My climbing partner greeted me at the terminal.

"I knew you'd be too tired for a three-day climbing trip, but don't worry. I've only planned a two-day one", she told me.

Friends were in from Colorado, I really had to go. A mere 1,000 vertical feet later, well into the Devil's Club and slide alder, the Coloradan peered at me through the wall-like vegetation. Though only 10 feet away I could barely make out her silhouette.

"Er, is this the kind of approach 'de rigeur' for the North Cascades?"

In fact we still had 3,000 more feet of the Devil to go, and it wasn't even raining yet. Folks from the lesser ranges sure do wimp out easily, I thought.

Can this trip be saved?

Conversation in the van now turned to food, one of my all-time favorable subjects. I asked the group, "How about an eating contest at the next Women Climber's Northwest climbing meet? You know, like the one's they write about in Climbing magazine."

This suggestion met with scowls of disapproval. Lana revived heself long enough to comment , "That's a terrible idea. You know how many women have problem with eating disorders. You'd just play to the worst side of women's psyches."

Alison seconded this opinion. "Yeah. I think that's a totally unhealthy idea. How about a beer drinking contest instead?"

"Yuck. How politically incorrect can you get?" remarked Jean.

Politically incorrect. Now there was an idea whose time was rampant. For example, politically correct skiing...thirteen years of conscientious face planting had not prepared me for the intricacies of this ethical philosophy.

It all began when Jean looked back over her shoulder at Margaret, diligently plodding up the slope behind us, and muttered, "Geez, she's ruining the line."

"Huh?" I inquired.

"Well, check it out girls, she's not following our tracks. She's makin' new ones that come right up the best line. Where's her ethics?"

I guessed Jean had a point, although later that day, and several arguments further along, I realized that we'd only scratched the surface of ski ethics. I stood, poised with fear, on the leading edge of what I believed to be a 5.11 face plastered with snow. I was so busy trying to remember how to calm my breath that I barely heard the directions shouted at me. (Do you count the in breaths or the out breaths?)

"Hey, Goldilocks, be SURE you eight my tracks!"

I ate her tracks? Huh? What had she said? Can I take up parachuting to save my ass on this Suredeathslope?

Full of questions I leapt through the cornice and poured down the slope. The slope ended up looking like a daisy chain with small pox, and I was soundly remonstrated for making far too many divots.

Can this trip be saved?

One thing all my friends agree about is that I am the local guru of bad taste. I swung the van into an IHOP for a caffeine refill and introduced my most promising social event of the week.

"Gang, this is it! A contest to see who can be the most politically incorrect! We'll have it at our April women's climbing meet--absolutely no holds barred."

Everyone had good ideas for entrants in this category. First of all we'd have it at the Peshastin Pinnacles, (now closed). Riding a three-wheeler up the sickly eroded trail to the base of the climbs would start the event off. Climbing in hair curlers, and a ghetto blaster with Barry Manilow at full volume were suggested. Of course an easily offensive entrant would be to bring a guy along, and it was clear that the grosser the guy the more points you'd rack up. I suggested seeing how many bolts we could fit on Porpoise, the classic 5.4 beginner's crack. At that point the girls decided we might have to have some kind of limits.

By now we were rolling up to the Canadian customs window and I thought of my last trip to Canada.

It's not everyone who'd choose to spend their vacation looking like a gortex bag lady. But, lo, I had heard the call of ice climbing. Alison and I had rounded up technical equipment from 17 of our closest climbing buddies, and buzzed up to Banff. Now Alison is the only northwest mountaineer who doesn't like to ski, but I assured myself it would help keep me off the fantastic Rockies powder and into the serious business of ice climbing. Four miles of postholding up a beautiful ski track to a frozen snot-like smear that was "just off the road," and I began to look around for another climbing partner.

Can this trip be saved?

Not to worry, two weeks in the Yosemite of Ice along the Banff-Jasper highway would not reveal a single other female ice maiden. "Sigh." But, learn to ice climb we did. Liz led on up the first day while I read aloud a technical article on how to place ice screws. Two weeks later our ropes looked like somebody had danced the flamenco in crampons on them, but we returned to

Seattle victorious and convinced that we had finally achieved the elusive quality of being true Hard Women.

I wheeled the van down the tiny lane and into the parking lot for Little Smoke Bluffs. Now came my least favorite part of any climbing trip. The repartee of the car was over, and the successful glow of having lead my first pitch was still a long way off. In between lay a wasteland of nervous chatter, gear sorting procrastination, and genuine always-harder-than-I-remembered-it, rock climbing. But I smiled to myself. Unlike most of the others in the van, I possessed the iron clad snobbism of a true northwest alpine climber. Someone who had put in the hard years of apprenticeship that I had learning techniques for brush, ice, snow, crevasses, bears, eight-month long rain would surely be excused a few muttered curses on a low-lying crag, being merely in training for the greater ranges.

Wendy Roberts is a biologist with a degree from Mt. Holyoke College in Massachusetts. She has recently taken up ice climbing with her adventures in the Canadian Rockies and an ascent of Mount Hunter's west ridge (northern spur). Her work as a biologist is far reaching, as she has studied alpine meadows in Colorado and is currently studying the behavior of seals in such locations as the Bering Sea and New Zealand.

Laura Waterman on High Exposure at the Shawangunks
Photo by Brad Snyder

When Women Were Women In The Northeast
Laura Waterman

Not long ago I went back to the Shawangunks. I walked the short path from the highway to the carriage road, as I had for the last 15 years. There was the usual throng of climbers bouldering, top-roping, and telling stories around the ranger's truck. I saw two women climbing "Apoplexy." Nearby, another woman was leading a man up "Retribution." These climbs are rated 5.9 and 5.10. Fifteen years ago people would have stopped to watch a man lead either climb. Now, in the mid-1980s, no one particularly noticed. Women were regularly leading hard climbs at the Gunks.

Yes, we've come a long way.

But these and other talented women climbers are simply re-establishing a tradition of women climbers that has a glorious past in northeastern rock climbing circles of more than 60 years ago.

Judged by the standard of their times--the only fair way to judge any climber--the women who climbed when climbing was first establishing itself in the Northeast were remarkable.

In the beginning was Miriam O'Brien Underhill. She has been called America's greatest woman climber.

"She was a beautiful climber, like an example from a climbing text," wrote New Englander Elizabeth Knowlton, a Himalayan veteran, and a contemporary who knew Miriam from her earliest climbing days. "Naturally graceful, she moved steadily and easily in rhythm, sort of flowing up the rocks. It was a pleasure to watch her."

Kenneth Henderson, an American alpinist of distinction, and good friend of Miriam's, unhesitatingly called her, "technically your top climber." He also pronounced her the only woman leader of her time.

Miriam climbed in New England, but she made her name in the Alps.

By the late 1920s and early 1930s, she had not only climbed many of the Alps' classic routes, but had begun to lead confidently herself on major routes without the services of a guide. In those days guideless climbing by women was frowned on.

In 1929 Miriam took a further step: she began a period of "manless" climbing, as an all-women's rope team was then called. For years she remained in the vanguard of a very small group of women who were doing manless ascents of difficult alpine peaks. Among her most notable climbs, major routes all of which were first ascents by a woman's rope, were the many-spired Grepon in 1929, the snow-and-ice covered Monch and Jungfrau in 1931, and the great massive pyramid of the irresistible Matterhorn, a real plum, a year later.

One might say that climbing without men (either guides or amateurs) in those days was just not done. In fact it was officially disapproved by the Ladies Alpine Club of London. Miriam wrote about this very controversial subject: "I have grown to recognize the fact that when a man lets a woman 'lead' it is, for him, just a pleasant little fiction...A woman cannot really lead if there is a man at all in the party...And so if she wants to lead she must climb with other women." She went on to say that if a man is in the party he will just naturally take over if an emergency arises; after all, what man, she wrote, "wouldn't feel a certain final responsibility when doing a climb with a woman? Call it illogical if you like, or perfectly natural, but I have tried out quite a lot of them, and they are all made that way." Miriam pointed out that during those years when she and a handful of other women pioneered on routes without men there never was an accident to a "manless caravan," of even a forced bivouac. But she was also aware that certain mothers who packed their daughters off for the Alps on a climbing holiday made them promise they "wouldn't climb with Miriam!"

Although Miriam did not happen to make her mark in the Northeast, several of her feminine contemporaries did--and did so just as the sport of rock climbing was beginning.

In 1928 four of the five big cliffs of the White Mountains in New Hampshire were climbed for the first time. It was a year, as historian Barbara Tuchman says of another era, "of vigor, confidence, and forces converging to quicken the blood." It proved but prologue: the following year saw even more spectacular advances, and major new climbs were racked up throughout the early 1930s from New Hampshire's vertical playgrounds to the cliff-bound mountains in Maine, back over to the comparatively isolated Adirondacks and down to the populated Hudson Highlands of New York. Women were along on many of these pioneering ascents.

Climbers from Boston opened up the White Mountain cliffs. Some of the women who were along on the earliest ascents included:

° *Marjorie Hurd, Boston lawyer, who said she climbed because she liked people and added, "The more strenuous the trip, the more interesting the people," was on the first attempt of the Pinnacle (direct) in Mt. Washington's Huntington Ravine in 1927.*

° *Jessie Whitehead, daughter of the famous philosopher Alfred North Whitehead, and noted for her ability, as Ken Henderson put it, to "push the leader up the rock with a good string of profanity," was on the team who finally climbed the Pinnacle (direct) in the Fall of 1928.*

° *Margaret Helburn, A Bostonian, who had an abiding love of mountains all her life, was with a party who explored far-off Katahdin's rock in 1928, led by Robert Underhill (Miriam's husband).*

By the early 1930s women were climbing every route which had been worked out by the pioneering Boston climbers on New England's cliffs:

° *Old Cannon on Cannon Cliff;*

° *Whitney-Gilman on Cannon;*

° *The south face of Willard in Crawford Notch;*

° *Huntington Ravine's Pinnacle;*

° *The Standard route on Whitehorse Ledge;*

° *The Standard route on Cathedral Ledge;*

° *Katahdin in Maine (many routes);*

° *Mount Desert in Maine (many routes).*

In the Adirondacks Betty Woolsey joined John Case to put up the first route on Wallface in 1933. A brilliant athlete, Betty successfully fused a life as a climber with that of a champion skier. She was on the U.S. Olympic women's ski team in the mid 1930s.

In 1935 fifteen Boston climbers went to Katahdin, under the able leadership of "Hec" Towle. In a week of climbing they put up eight new routes and the Armadillo was the prize, a long, complex route in the middle of the cirque called the South Basin. Not technically hard--Towle's route was about 5.5--the exposure and overall length as well as the remoteness of the cliff put it right up with the explorations done on New Hampshire rock of a few years earlier. On one day five of the men explored it and completed the route. Two days later, after waiting out a rain, 12 climbers did the route! Four of them were women, including Thelma Bonney, (later Towle when she married "Hec"), Marjorie Hurd, Helen Chase, and Gretchen Cleaves, all well-known in the Boston and Appalachian Mountain Club climbing circle.

In this age when we all pay meticulous attention to the ratings of climbs, and even 5.13 is subdivided (5.13a, 5.13b, 5.13c, 5.13d...), it is difficult to place ourselves back in the context of the 1930s. Then there were no ratings. If you were a rock climber, you climbed all the routes. So any really active woman climbed just about everything the men climbed. In those days of hemp rope and genuine commitment in leading, few climbers led. That's where a sex gap developed: few women led. But in climbing per se, there was not the large gap between men and women which developed during the 1950s and 1960s. Thus, Marjorie Hurd, and Jessie Whitehead on pioneering New Hampshire climbs, Betty Woolsey on the first ascent of Wallface, Thelma Bonney on the second ascent of the Armadillo.

This historical fact is little realized today. We all tend to think that the achievements of Lynn Hill and other women who climb as well as men today are unprecedented. These achievements *are* indeed impressive, because of the mental roadblocks and prejudices of the last generation which had to be cleared away. But in the early days a greater degree of parity had existed. A look at the historical development of one eastern area, the Shawangunks, is revealing.

As every climber knows, the Gunks were discovered in 1935, sighted in the clear air that follows a thundershower by Fritz Wiessner from the top of Breakneck Ridge. And so began the era of modern rock climbing.

A close look at the climbing history of the Shawangunks, the East's most prominent rock climbing center, reveals a startling fact: for that area at least, *more women were climbing at the top of the prevailing standard in the 1940s and 1950s than at any time since then.*

A careful perusal of three guidebooks (Art Gran's was published in 1964 and Dick Williams' in 1972 and Todd Swain's in 1986) reveals that women were particularly active in first ascents during the 1940s. In the 1950s the number of routes put up nearly doubled, and the number of women involved in them stayed the same. During the 1960s the number of new routes again doubled, whereas the number of women climbers on first ascents dwindled markedly.

There have, of course, always been women climbers at the Gunks, some of whom led at the top of *their* standard. But the following breakdown is in terms of men and women who have been involved in first ascents only, as this information can be documented by the guidebooks.

1940-1950 : The total number of documented climbs put in was 63. A total of 32 of these had women in the party--or 51 percent.

1951-1959 : In these years the total number of documented new climbs nearly doubled to 109. The number of climbs with women in the party stayed the same at 32, so the percentage of total number of climbs which included women was nearly cut in half--29 percent.

1960-1970 : The total number of reported new routes more than doubled--221. The number of climbs with women in the party decreased to just 11 climbs, reducing the percent to a low of 5 percent.

1971-1979 : In the explosion of climbing's popularity, 561 new routes were recorded. Though the number involving women doubled, to 21, their percentage remained low: 4 percent.

1980-1985 : With 683 new routes entered in the guidebook, and 63 involving women, the proportion began its slow return toward earlier levels: 9 percent for the first half of this decade.

Who were these women participating in just about half the new routes climbed during the 1940s and early 1950s?

To begin at the beginning, in 1935 the very first route put up at the Gunks was Old Route at Milbrook, and a female, Peggy Navas was in the party led by Fritz Wiessner.

Among the top climbers of the early days at the Shawangunks --men or women-- a name that stands out right after Hans Kraus and Fritz Wiessner, who really opened up the area, is Bonnie Prudden.

Physical fitness crusader and sometime television star, Bonnie Prudden was from the late Thirties to the mid Fifties a rock climber extraordinaire. She climbed all over the Northeast, in the West (the Tetons and Estes Park), and in Europe, especially the Dolomites.

Hans Kraus, a dominant early figure at the Shawangunks, recalls her as "the best woman climber in the area." If you look through the list of climbs in Williams' 1972 guidebook, Kraus' verdict gains support. The star-studded names of Jim McCarthy, Williams, Kraus, Gran, and Wiessner are the men who put in the most numbers of new routes at the Gunks. Then comes Bonnie Prudden.

Bonnie has a documented thirty first ascents taking place in the years 1946 to 1955. Among these is the famed Bonnie's Roof, rated 5.8. (Gran's guide and many a dangling leader rate it a 5.9.) Bonnie put in the route with Kraus and she led the roof, using a sling for aid. This was in 1952. The aid was not eliminated until 1961, when McCarthy and Williams managed to climb the big ceiling free. The route remains a testpiece for climbers breaking into a higher standard. Gran writes in his guidebook, "It's a great route to bear one's name."

Among Bonnie's other notable climbs are Something Interesting, a tough 5.7 put in at the early date of 1946. Grand Central came the following year. In 1951 she climbed with Hans Kraus Never Again, rated 5.6a$_1$, at the time, and today goes free at solid 5.10. That year she and Hans climbed Hans' Puss , a truly fine route and one of the longest at the Gunks. Triangle followed in 1954 and Dry Martini a year later. Aside from documented climbs, Bonnie recalls many nameless routes at Lost City (which she remembers being called "Secret City") and other outlying crags. The hardest free moves on these climbs were respectful 5.7, done at a time no one was climbing 5.8.

Bonnie holds a place in the climbing history of the Shawangunks that has yet to be superceded by any other woman climber, especially in terms of her first ascents, in leading climbs at the top of her standard--in fact at the top of the standard of the area--she was unique among women climbers of her day. Only with the advent of the remarkable Lynn Hill in the early 1980s has any woman approached Bonnie's challenge. The climbers of Bonnie's time remember her vividly, describing her as "tops" or "the best", among all women climbers. Bonnie was a luminary in the climbing scene for more than a decade.

Krist Raubenheimer was a potent force at the Shawangunks in the mid Fifties. An aggressive leader on many of the area's then-harder routes, Krist also put in several first ascents of her own, which ranks her right behind Bonnie among women pioneers, though a long way down the list among the men.

Krist put up some very fine climbs. Among them, The Raubenheimers Special was rated 5.5 in Williams' guide, but it's a rating many climbers felt hardly did the climb justice when they were clinging desperately to that utterly blank crux. At least 5.6! Swain's guide moved it up to that rating. Krist is also responsible for the very popular Bunny (5.4) which she climbed with Ann Church--an all female climb, one of the very few at the Shawangunks.

Although Krist does not really come close to Bonnie Prudden in her number of first ascents, she was as good as there was and Hans Kraus recalls her as next best among the women climbers. She, like Bonnie, led climbs at the top of her standard.

Back in the Forties, another woman climber whose reputation stands high in the memory of old timers in the area, is Maria Millar. Although the marvelous route that bears her name is one of just two first ascents of hers in the guidebook, she is recalled as a capable leader on the harder established routes of the day. The intensely competitive Bonnie Prudden once said, "I never met another woman other than Maria Millar who could really climb."

Maria was a born climber. Before she discovered rocks she climbed water towers, traversed churches, chimneyed doorways, climbed balconies on hotels, climbed over slowly moving freight trains, and of course, climbed houses and trees. At the Gunks she is remembered--now only by the oldest of old timers--as a brilliant natural climber, sparked by tremendous enthusiasm and spirit.

The climbers of the Shawangunks owe a lot to Maria, as it was she, and her husband David, who took Hans Kraus to the Gunks for the first time.

Mary Perry and Del Wolcott each have five first ascents to their credit, though neither are remembered as leading at the level of Bonnie or Maria.

Betty Woolsey, who was with Fritz Wiessner and Bill House on Mount Waddington, also put in four new routes at the Gunks in the early Forties. Among them the classic jam crack "The Baby" is rated 5.6 and was put up in 1941 by Fritz Wiessner, Betty Woolsey, and Mary Cecil. The popular beginner's route, The Betty, memorializes Ms. Woolsey, who put it in also in the same year. She is remembered as being a very competent climber.

Ann Church was on three first ascents, two of which were put up with Krist Raubenheimer in 1955, making them the first all-female rope doing first ascents at the Shawangunks.

Ruth Tallan is one whom Maria Millar remembers as a climber of natural grace and skill who developed into one of the area's better climbers, and eventually chairman (this was before the years of "consciousness raising" terminology like "chairperson") of the dominant club climbing at the Gunks, the Appalachian Mountain Club.

Dorothy Hirschland was another who did outstanding climbs and also led at a respectable standard for the times.

These were the outstanding female leaders of the Forties and Fifties, although many other women were active in the then-smaller climbing circle at the Shawangunks. By the end of the Fifties and the early Sixties, women were far less prominent either in making first ascents or leading at the demanding new standards then being pushed by McCarthy, Gran, Williams and others.

Why the change? Why were women so much more active at the forefront of Gunks' climbing in the early days? Here are a few conjectures.

1. The climbing population was small, not more than 10 to 25 climbers on a weekend, and more like 8 to 10 climbers in the early days of the Forties. A reasonably high proportion of these climbers were women; certainly a much higher proportion than are found at the cliffs today when a pleasant, sunny weekend will bring out hundreds of climbers at the height of the season.

2. Somehow the social scene in those days was conducive to women leading and following climbs near the top of the standard for the area. The small number of climbers at the Gunks might have contributed. Also, everyone knew each other. This, as well as the fact that climbing then was not unduly competitive seems to have produced a context in which women could advance.

3. The Appalachian Mountain Club, the dominant group at the Shawangunks during the Forties and Fifties employed a system of advancing leaders that was rather formal and restrictive, but at least had the merit that it did not discriminate between male or female. In fact, as mentioned, Ruth Tallan served as chairman of this group for a time.

4. Hans Kraus and Fritz Wiessner, who put up many, many first ascents liked to climb with women. Hans was happy to have women lead. Fritz liked to have women along in his party, so often one or two women's names accompany his in his roster of first ascents.

Reasons unique to the Shawangunks, however, are probably not a sufficient explanation of the prominence of women climbers in the early days, because other Northeastern climbing areas, as we have seen, show a similar leading role by women during the Twenties and Thirties. In fact by the Forties, Jan Conn was putting in routes like the very serious Conn Course on Cannon Cliff, in which she alternated leads with her partner Herb Conn. The first Adirondacks' rock climbing guidebook was written by a woman, Trudy Healy, who knew as well as anyone cliffs large and small of that region.

Yet some time in the Fifties there was a definite diminuendo in the role of women climbers in the Northeast. The statistics on first ascents at the Shawangunks, cited earlier, gave dramatic evidence of this change. What might be some of the reasons?

1. After 1960 the average difficulty of first ascents increased to 5.8/5.9, and in the 1970s many of the old aid routes were freed, most going at 5.10 and harder. Generally, women just hadn't convinced themselves, at this point, that they could climb at that level. Very likely the strenuous nature of the climbs put them off.

2. After 1960 and particularly in the Seventies, climbing became more competitive than it was in the more relaxed early years. Possibly, this predominantly male competition that goes on at the upper end of the standard drives out the women climbers. Vera Watson, a former Gunks climber who was a team member of the all-women expedition to Annapurna in 1978, commented that she had done much of her climbing with women and found "more of a feeling of camaraderie, less competitiveness."

3. The climbing population has increased markedly since the 1940s and 1950s. The increase had brought many more male climbers than female to the cliffs, thus reducing the chances that women climbers would be on first ascents.

4. One old Vulgarian (these were the climbers who were setting standards during the early Sixties) maintained that Vulgarians liked to have women around for other purposes than strictly climbing...(Several of the women who were climbing during this period don't support this point, however, as they claim that these men encouraged them in their climbing).

In the Sixties and early Seventies there were certainly good women climbers at the Gunks. Several of these women were doing harder climbs than Bonnie Prudden and Krist Raubenheimer, but the standard of climbing had increased so fast during the Sixties that in retrospect their climbing seems not as impressive as that of their predecessors. So that although these climbers were doing free moves that Bonnie or Krist never attempted, they were climbing at a level far behind the standard set by the men.

Gerd Thuestad, who climbed at the Shawangunks from 1950 to 1969, led all of Vulga-tits (5.6), put in by an all-female party. Gerd also did a lot of leading and at the top of her standard. She climbed a lot with women, and remembers getting into very funny situations on her all-female climbs. Muriel Mayo did some very capable leading, including a first ascent of After You (rated 5.7).

Patty Crowther and Cherry Merritt were two women who were leading hard climbs. Cherry led Art Gran's classic thin-face climb Never Never Land rated 5.10 by Gran and 5.9 by Williams and Swain.

But these women were exceptions to the trend. Despite the impetus of the "Women's Movement" emerging in the 1960s, most women climbers were leading far below their standard. None was following at the highest standard of the men.

The 1970s, though backward in many ways, saw the first signs of change. Women were climbing more with other women--and not just on the easy grades, but at a moderately hard level. In 1977 *Mountain* reported, "Another development [at the Shawangunks] has been the appearance of increasing numbers of competent women climbers, operating at the top grades." This well-known British climbing magazine went on to name Barbara Devine as "the most successful of the female climbers." Climber-historian Al Rubin commented that by the mid-Seventies he noticed a definite increase in good women climbers, and that women were climbing together more.

The *wunderkind* of the Seventies was without doubt Barbara Devine. She stepped into the vacuum left by the Sixties, and, with no female role models for inspiration, worked her way up to the stratosphere of the highest grades, becoming herself a model for her followers.

Barbara began climbing in 1970. She was taken to the Gunks by her boyfriend Kevin Bein--a Gunks habitue'--who proceeded to drag her up Northern Pillar (5.2). Terrified, Barbara resolved never to climb again. But the idea of overcoming her fear took hold, and she returned to the cliffs for another try. Barbara Devine came to stay. Two years later she accompanied Kevin to Yosemite and did her first 5.9s. In 1973 (now married) the couple moved to New Paltz and became probably the most constant presences at the cliffs; climbing "literally every day," training intensively, bouldering hard, and striving constantly to improve their standards. Tall and thin, Barbara developed a phenomenal strength-to-weight ratio (she has especially strong fingers) when she took up serious training. By 1974 she led Retribution, possibly the first female lead of solid 5.10 in Northeastern climbing. That was just the beginning. By 1976, she had done Foops and Persistent, both

5.11. In 1977 she did Kansas City (5.12) and such desperate 5.11s as Open Cockpit, To Have Or Have Not, and Wasp Stop. Barbara was moving fast. In July 1983 she did the first female ascent of Supercrack, plus other 5.12s of that day. Like her husband, Barbara was always subjected to an under-current of whispers about poor style -- willingness to accept a top-rope, lengthy sieging, and a preference for nearby protection on leads. For sheer technical virtuosity, however, there was no denying that she was far and away the outstanding woman climber in the Northeast during the 1970's.

A top climber of the Eighties, Rosie Andrews, said of Barbara that in the late Seventies "Barbara Devine was perhaps the best-known woman who had done hard climbs in the East." Rosie pointed out that Barbara is an example of what women can do --and yet still be limited. Technically she was impeccable, but she was possibly not willing enough to step out on her own, since she rarely climbed outside of her husband Kevin's circle--all brilliant climbers, but predominantly men.

By the Eighties, women were willing to step out on their own.

By about 1980 Iza Koponicka, a graceful climber with superb technique was leading 5.9s and occasionally 5.10s. Annie O'Neill and Laura Chaiten were right up there too. These women, though, were not leading (or even following) at the top of the area's standard as was Bonnie Prudden.

But perhaps the next woman after Barbara with a substantial independent impact on female climbing was Rosie Andrews. Rosie took striking out on one's own seriously. By 1980 she was leading consistently in the 5.10 range and had moved up to the thinner air of 5.11 by 1981. Unlike many other strong women climbers at that time, Rosie never really had her name linked with that of a strong male climber. Once she got good, she seemed to maintain a kind of independence that was possibly unique among Eastern women climbers. By doing this, she became an extremely effective role model.

Rosie comes close to being the first woman since Bonnie Prudden to put in the climbs at the area's standard. In 1981 she stunned the Gunks community by leading a crux 5.12 move on a first ascent of Point Blank with Russ Raffa. Though Russ ultimately first led the entire climb, word got around about Rosie leading that one desperate move.

Rosie led a growing movement toward more independent self-contained women climbers in the early 1980s. She was the first woman to guide professionally in the East, working for International Mountain Equipment in North Conway, N.H. in 1982. In the mid 1980s she guided at the Gunks, influencing many women to "strike out on their own." Her landmark article on women climbers published in *Mountain* in 1984 was avidly devoured.

Another climber of independent mind was Alison Osius. A journalist whose sage and amusing articles appear often in the climbing press, she is at home leading 5.12.

In 1983 a 21-year-old slight, slender, attractive California woman came East. Lynn Hill had been a gymnast, swimmer, and hiker from childhood. Gifted with uncommon strength, but even more flexibility and grace, she took to rock climbing with ease. Before she left California, she had climbed 5.12. But when she arrived in the Northeast, her climbing activity level, physical fitness, competitive instincts, and mental attitude came together to make her a top-flight climber. Not a top-flight woman climber; simply a top-flight climber. In 1983 she was one of four Gunks climbers to master the region's first 5.13, Vandals. In 1984, making one of her few trips to North Conway to sample local test-pieces, she took on Tourist Treat, a problem which had been stumping local climbers for years; she led it on sight, with but one fall, perhaps the most difficult first ascent in the north country at the time. In the same year, back at the Gunks, she led the first ascents of Organic Iron (5.12 plus) and the original aid line on Yellow Crack (5.12 plus with scant protection), the latter called by Russ Raffa, himself a 5.12 leader with a reputation for boldness: "the best lead I've ever seen in my life." When the 1986 guidebook was published, the cover photo unselfconsciously showed Lynn Hill leading Open Cockpit. That long-time observer of the Gunks scene, Kevin Bein, pronounced her, in 1986: "the best climber in the Gunks now." Most observers declined to set any one of the seven or eight top 1980s climbers ahead of the rest, but the point was clear that no man was climbing significantly better than Lynn Hill. Bonnie Prudden's long-awaited heiress had arrived at last.

Though cited here as exceptional "women climbers," these women of the 1980s were beginning to think of themselves simply as "climbers." The distinction was significant. Rosie Andrews, Alison Osius, Lynn Hill and others vehemently disclaimed special recognition as women and sought to be accepted as climbers. Their example spread. Alison insisted, after a first free ascent of the Labyrinth Wall on Cannon Cliff, with three pitches at 5.11 and six at 5.10, wherein she shared the lead with Neil Cannon: "There's no intrinsic reason why women can't climb as well as men. So we shouldn't get congratulated for lesser accomplishments."

Women had caught up. Actually, only Lynn Hill. The general level of female climbing was still well below males'. But clearly barriers had been removed, and it appeared unlikely that another "dark ages" could return. The new outlook owed much to the path-breaking by Barbara Devine, Rosie Andrews, Alison Osius and Lynn Hill, but the real story written in the 1980s was by the anonymous multitude of women who climbed well and independently, perceiving themselves once again in the mainstream of northeastern climbing.

Laura Waterman began climbing in 1969 at the Shawangunks and is best known for the first woman ascent of the Cannon's "Black Dike" one of the most challenging ice Climbing routes in the Eastern United States. Her accomplishments as an ice climber merits her the adjective "best" in the field.

Laura Waterman now lives with her husband in the State of Vermont . They published **F orest Craig- A History of Climbing, Trailblazing in the North Eastern Mountains,** *and are working on another volume on the history of the area's rock and ice climbing.*

Recollections Of Margaret
Annie Whitehouse

I miss Margaret in her baggy pants and loose cotton shirt, pockets heavy with her altimeter, note cards and pencil. For those who knew Margaret Young, that image alone will bring a smile and stir memories of shared adventures and climbs. For those who didn't, I hope to recall the curious and pioneering nature of a very special woman.

My desire for 5.12 and high mountain ascents began with my association with Margaret. Picture a sixteen year old girl, sturdy and able, offered the opportunity to fly over the Sierra Nevada in a Cessna 180 piloted by this enigmatic woman and then to climb the steep couloir of the North Palisade in January. I had been climbing some at that time. I was both excited and intimidated, for until that time I had the vague notion that climbing was a group undertaking. Under the insightful and keen tutelage of Phil Arnot and David Lunn I was taught basics of climbing through a high school class. Instead of studying the 3-R's we were often out climbing, en masse, in various locations throughout the Western states.

We were to meet at her house for an early morning start. Grey metal shelves lined the entrance, on which were stacked pitons, ice screws, fossils, airplane parts, a dog food dish, dusty pieces of wood, books and various manuals. Advancing further I noticed an automatic chart of the elements taped to one of the kitchen walls, under which she sat. She was on the telephone getting a pilot briefing for our flight. She scribbled the flight information directly onto her kitchen table in what seemed to me to be a confusing mess of abbreviations, elevations and arrows.

I stood and watched, thinking that her kitchen looked more like a laboratory; nesting sets of measuring cups, metal bowls and labeled plastic containers on metal shelves. The sun had not yet risen, but if it had, little light would have come in. Black spray-painted 10 gallon plastic water containers sat on even more metal shelves in front on the south facing windows. These, she later told me, were an experiment in solar heating. As I think back, I realize Margaret's house was not the chaotic array of things it might have seemed, but an efficient work space. The out of doors; clean, pure and ordered by nature was where she seemed to feel at home.

As a novice climber I was only too eager to charge up a mountain, oblivious to the world around me. This was not Margaret's approach. Margaret liked to dream up the most improbable, outrageous schemes and then carry them out with meticulous attention to detail. The continuity of her approach became more tangible as we drove to the airport. The high cirrus clouds above us in Palo Alto were an integral part of the weather projection, she repeated to me. Not only did they mean high winds aloft for our flight, but they indicated high pressure and possible windy conditions for our climb.

The entire plane shaked and shuddered as she revved the engine during the preflight inspection. I sat, buckled in, looking out the window at our small red and white airplane's little tires. They belonged on a toy car rather than a plane. Blind faith and naivety abound in youth!

Once up she asked me if I wanted to fly for awhile. Over the roar of the engine I learned how the rudders, yoke and ailerons worked. She shouted, "If you want to go left, push in on the left rudder and turn the yoke to the left at the same time. To go up pull the yoke towards you, and to go down, push it in. O.K., now fly at this elevation and keep the heading indicator at 170°." I was sure we were going to get hit by a Greyhound bus. She gazed out the window, jotting down numbers on the aero chart held in her lap. My neck and shoulders felt as though they would turn to stone. I knew that the Greyhound bus was out there somewhere. She took the controls back over Fresno. By then I was kind of having fun.

We landed, tied down quickly and called a friend to give us a ride to the road's end. As we approached the North Palisade, Margaret's slow, steady pace was occasionally interrupted to photograph snow, delicately balanced on a branch or to ponder the geologic events leading to the rock formations we passed.

Last fall while climbing in the Schwangunks I felt something remiss. Many days we parked our car alongside the road, walked along the carriage road to the base of the climb and then climbed. Many climbers, including myself, seemed oblivious to their environment. Only the powerful pull of the cliffs held our attention. In Margaret's world both the climbing and the surroundings would have intrigued her. I can picture her questioning the climbing ranger at the Uberfalls about where one can legally camp, what kind of trees were those and how many climbers paid fees today?

Margaret was introduced to climbing in the Schwangunks. During the early 1950's she studied physics and chemistry at the Massachusetts Institute of Technology (M.I.T.) On weekends and school breaks she joined the M.I.T. outing club's sojourns to the "Gunk's" wild overhangs, finding a pleasure and niche in climbing. Later she moved to Palo Alto, California for both its proximity to the mountains and its growing scientific community.

The industrious climbing section of the Sierra Club offered Margaret climbing partners and opportunities for challenging climbs. When I joined Margaret on a Sierra Club climb I sensed her fellow climbers were both amused and respectful of her indomitable nature. The more complicated the approach and the less straightforward the climb, the more Margaret seemed to enjoy herself. Being the impetuous, on trips ranging from the first winter ascent of 14,000' Mt. Tyndall to a more imaginative Trans-Sierra winter crossing on snowshoes, her reputation as a strong-willed, determined climber was firmly established.

A July 27, 1968 Palo Alto Times article reads, "A doctor, a student, two scientists and a homemaker[!?]. Put them together and what do you get? A mountain climbing team...en route right now where they will climb Chimborazo and Cotopaxi. Being the only woman in the party does not faze Mrs. Young. "I have been on quite a few climbs as the only woman. Besides, you can never tell who you will meet on the mountain."

Margaret found being a woman and a climber easily congruent. I adopted that attitude without question, besides you can never tell who you will meet on the mountain. I recall meeting skiers swooshing through the powder snow of the Bugaboos while Vera Watson, Margaret and I plodded across the cirque on snowshoes after climbing S. Hauser Tower in subzero temperatures. They seemed surprised to see three women with heavy packs walking through the knee deep powder. They refused my offer of trading their skis for some used climbing equipment and a frustrating pair of snowshoes. Having accomplishments under or overrated because I am female seems odd and unnecessary. Certainly there are differences between men and women. To objectively recognize those differences and to climb using individual talents only makes sense.

Though there has always been rivalries and rule setting in climbing, Margaret has unfortunately missed the controversies

present today. To Margaret climbing was not in need of a definition. A climb was defined by the skill and objectives of the person
climbing. You usually started from the bottom and did what you
wanted to do to reach the top. Or started from the top, as she did
when making her "Glen Canyon first and last ascents". In this case
they started from the rim of the canyon, rapelled down and rafted
along the base of the cliffs as the waters in Glen Canyon rose.
Several "first and last ascents" were made and captured on film as
the climbers ascended the now underwater sandstone walls in the
bluff.

I am certain that Margaret would find some of the controversies interesting and worthy of thought, but not to be solved in
concrete terms. She valued the individualistic nature of climbing
far too much to be obliged to follow other's rules and opinions. A
progressive thinker, Margaret would have been delighted to trade
her black polyester climbing pants in for a pair of green and pink
lycra and give hangdogging a shot.

In 1963 Margaret flew her Cessna to Alaska. The unclimbed
S.E. ridge of Foraker and Moose's Tooth were her objectives.
Unsuccessful in reaching the summit of both, she returned the next
year to the virtually unexplored area of 'Little Switzerland' southwest of McKinley to make several first ascents. Later she returned
to climb the S. Moose's Tooth, this also being a first ascent.
Climbs in Bolivia, Nepal, Afghanistan, Russia and Africa were
interspersed with her frequent trips to the Sierras.

Determination was one of Margaret's strong points. Something I learned early climbing with her was that given halfway
decent conditions you can usually get to the top by just keeping
going. On Noshaq in 1972 she set the altitude record for American
women by climbing it in her "own alpine style." She and Bill
Griffin set out to climb the west ridge one day after she arrived at
base camp. Seven days later she arrived at the summit solo. Her
climbing partner turned back because of cold feet. Arlene Blum,
the leader of this expedition, described Margaret as careful, but
unconventional. She refused to abide by Arlene's plan of climbing in expedition style, preferring to slowly acclimatize by
ascending in a slow, focused manner.

Margaret was dead by the time I joined the 1983 American
expedition to climb Everest's west ridge. She died of cancer after
a horseback accident left her partially paralyzed. The day Renny
Jackson, Eric Reynolds and I ascended the Hornbein Couloir in
hope of attaining Everest's summit was cold and clear. The hills

and valleys of Tibet, muted shades of brown and pink, were far below. We were above even the surrounding icy white Himalayan peaks. Each laborious step drew me upward, wanting to take another. Sometimes vivid recollections of Margaret, her solid determination and spirit, spurred me on. The two cold oxygenless nights we spent at 27,000' were uncomfortable and at times scary. Again, thoughts of Margaret among other fleeting recollections of life and loved ones kept me going. She probably would have enjoyed it up there.

I appreciate the introduction Margaret gave me to climbing. Sometimes I wonder, what is this thing called "climbing", a quest or an obsession? What is this thing that takes my body and mind, shapes and molds it, giving and taking strength? My answer will change, but the mountains, rocks and plants I pass along the way will not.

Annie Whitehouse is recognized as one of America's foremost female expedition climbers. In 1983 she set the American women's altitude record by reaching 28,000 feet on Everest's west ridge. She has been a member of an expedition to the north face of Mount Everest and was on the 1978 all women expedition to Annapurna. She has contributed articles to National Geographic and Outside Magazines.

Elizabeth D. Woolsey

Annie Whitehouse   Photo by Karl Horak

Early Climbs
Elizabeth D. Woolsey

My first climbing adventure came close to ending in tragedy. I was thirteen when I wandered off from a school picnic in Mt. Carmel near New Haven, and followed a path that skirted the base of a cliff. Impulsively, I decided to climb it.

The climb went easily the first few feet, gradually grew more difficult until I was stopped by a holdless section some thirty feet off the ground. I then discovered that it's easier to climb up than down. I was spread-eagled there for what seemed like hours; my muscles began to cramp, my legs to shake; my heart pounded and although it was a cool, fall day, I was drenched in sweat.

I held on for agonizing minutes and then fell off backwards. I remember nothing of the fall itself and landed in a bushy evergreen tree, the only one growing from the rocks of the talus slope. I crashed on down to the ground, landing on a bed of broken branches, twigs and needles. I had cuts and bruises, but no broken bones and my faith in my guardian angel was unshaken.

This accident in no way dampened my interest in climbing, though being stiff and sore I temporarily became an armchair mountaineer. I read Frederic Burlingham's How to Become An Alpinist in which it became apparent that he greatly admired the women climbers of his day. Of Mrs. Bullock Workman he writes, "The American, not long ago ascended to the tremendous height of 23,300 feet in the Nun Kun Range in Kashmir as she has been eight times in the Himalayas it would not surprise her friends to read, almost any morning that she is at it again."

From an account of the second ascent of Mt. Blanc by a woman, Mlle. d'Angeville, he has this to say, "Owing to the rarefied air she sank down exhausted . . . by pure will power she ordered the caravan to proceed, and exclaimed, 'Promise me that if I die on the way you will carry me to the top.'" Burlingham reassures his readers that the lady did, in fact, reach the top alive and "after dancing a quadrille in the snow at 15,781 feet she said she wanted to go higher than Mt. Blanc, and climbed on the shoulders of the guides. Enthusiasm such as this will lead one almost anywhere."

We have little clue as to what Miss Annie Peck, the conqueror of Mt. Huascaran, in Peru, really looked like as there is not an inch of skin exposed in her studio portrait. A floppy hat is pulled down over her forehead and she is wearing a face mask over goggles. Her laced boots reach the knee and bloomer-like knickers end above them. The space between is covered by what appears to be long, white underwear.

Although I had lived in the shadow of the mountains for many years it wasn't until I was 15 that I got above tree line on a trip to Europe with the Winslows, the parents of a classmate, Nancy. I was promised that after a certain amount of educational sightseeing we would go to the Pyrenees and then on the Geneva, where Dr. Winslow was due to present a paper before the League of Nations.

I kept a diary with fairly equal space devoted to food (generally not to my liking), to museums, castles and other historic sites. In Les Baux, for example, which I admired for its fortifications, perched on a limestone crag high above the valley, I comment, "Had the worst dinner of my life, with dishwater soup, then omelet saturated in kerosene. The climax was a stringy chicken, with head attached."

Dr. Winslow remembered his promise about climbing and sent Mrs. Winslow ahead to Gavarni with the luggage when we left Biarritz. He, Nancy and I hiked to the Lac Du Gaube where we would spend the night before traversing the Vignemale, some 3,298 meters, coming into Gavarni on the far side of the mountain. Our guide woke us before sunrise and the route started with easy mountain walking. Then, "We had some exciting times crossing deep snow on the almost perpendicular side of the mountain . . ." I was exaggerating, but this was my first mountain and I was only fifteen.

Shortly after our arrival in Geneva we motored to Chamonix where I was impressed by the great peaks and aiguilles--or sheer rocky spires-- of the French Alps rising just outside town. The streets were full of mountaineering types and, through a telescope set up in the town square, I watched a group struggling through deep snow on their descent of Mt. Blanc. Lunching on the terrace at Montenvers, overlooking the Mer du Glace, I saw a threesome that was to have a profound influence on my life, a slender, sunburned woman, quite old I decided (probably around thirty), with two men all in nail boots and carrying rucksacks, ropes and ice axes. They were handsome, vital and about to head for unknown adventures in the mountains. I was suddenly overcome by a desperate longing to become a member, some day, of such a party. This, I now realize, was a turning point in my life.

Back in New Haven I found my first climbing companions, the Whitney brothers, both undergraduates at Yale. Roger, the older brother was tall and blond, Hassler equally tall and red-headed. Both were good climbers and excellent teachers. From them I learned how to handle the rope; methods of belaying, and how to pendule. We practiced long, free rappels from the "Nose" of the Sleeping Giant, which involved placing a doubled climbing rope around a solid object such as a tree or a rocky knob and sliding down it. The rope could then be retrieved at the foot of the cliff by pulling down one end. The Mt. Carmel cliffs were of no great extent, but had enough variety for practice in chimney and crack climbing as well as friction climbing on smooth slabs. My next sister, Anne, about my size, joined us on many of the climbs and did very well.

My father gave me a climbing rope for Christmas and I took it along to New Mexico in 1927 where Anne and I met Ashley Pond and George Massey, also friends from Yale. Our first climb was to the top of the Enchanted Mesa, a steep-sided, flat-topped butte west of Albuquerque in the Acoma Indian Reservation. We followed a relatively easy route via a series of chimneys, finding solid wooden pegs pounded into the rock cracks that could be used as hand holds. On top we admired the view of the ancient village of Acoma, perched on its own high mesa and still inhabited, and decided to take another way down.

As we had my 120 foot climbing rope, we decided to descend a sheer side in a series of rappels. The top section went well as we found a ledge every 40 feet or so with a convenient knob to anchor the rope and repeat the procedure. But the last pitch above the valley floor was much further than my rope would reach. We couldn't climb up as we'd come down over a series of overhangs and were in a jackpot.

It was blisteringly hot on our unsheltered ledge; we had no water and were in a remote area (in those days) of the Acoma Indian Reservation. The ledge we were trapped on continued around the face of the mesa ending in a sheer cliff.

Without much hope--but it was better than just sitting and waiting for complete dehydration--I followed the ledge and found that there was a chimney between the cliff and our shelf which had been hidden from sight until I was directly above it. There, hanging down and reaching all the way to the ground, was a rope, possibly left by climbers who had found themselves in the same predicament that we were in. A shout brought my companions to my side. We tested the rope; it was solid and we were soon all down on the valley floor. I have always been grateful to our unknown saviours--and to my guardian angel.

Although Mesa Verde had been made a National Park in 1906, it was still largely undeveloped and unexplored in 1927. The four of us borrowed camping equipment from the Ponds who lived in Santa Fe, stocked the car with food and headed north to Colorado, following the New Mexican-Colorado border until just before the Four Corners, where Arizona, Utah, Colorado and New Mexico touch. There we turned south on the road leading to the top of the plateau where park headquarters were located.

Anne and I pitched our tent near the rim of the mesa with a wonderful view over the deep canyons that lead from the plateau. We found several eccentric characters camped there who had preceded us. There was a lady dressed in Chinese clothes who spent most of her time sitting on a log playing a flute. Another had her sleeping bag laid out on a narrow ledge, protected by an overhang of rock. Rumor had it that a magnificent mountain lion came to curl up beside her every night, taking off at dawn. Anne and I inspected the eyrie while the lady was away, and were delighted to find the pad marks of a big cat in the dirt under some nearby cedar trees.

We were given permission to explore the park as long as we left all undisturbed in the cliff dwellings that it contained. We would pack a lunch, fill our canteens with water, and spend the days hiking and climbing. We found many cliff dwellings, most of them perched high above the floor of the canyons. These we would climb up to from below when possible, or rappel down into them from above, using trees to anchor our ropes. We spent a tense hour under a great vaulted niche, full of broken pottery and bones, during a violent cloudburst while the lightning flickered around us and the thunder reverberated from the canyon walls.

My first chance at real mountaineering came the summer of 1928 when Anne and I were sent to Europe with Alice Lowell, of Boston, as chaperone. It was not an ideal arrangement as Anne and I (or was it chiefly I?) wanted to be in the mountains and Alice preferred the Salzburg Festival where she had a chance to sing in the chorus.

After a walking trip in the Black Forest we arrived in Salzburg where I found a letter from the Whitney boys waiting for me. They suggested that Anne and I meet them in Switzerland for some climbing. I immediately cabled my father for permission and the answer was "Certainly." This reply was no surprise as father had always been supportive of my climbing, indeed had given me my first rope. I suspect that he found life as a consulting forester a bit quiet in contrast to the challenges of his early years as a ranger in New Mexico and the service overseas with the American Expeditionary Forces in World War I. I am sure that he took pleasure in listening to my own tales which evidently evoked memories of his own active years.

The Whitneys and their cousin Bradley Gilman (who became the president of the American Alpine Club in 1953) met us in Montreux and we immediately headed up into the Alps Vaudoises for training climbs, sleeping in various alpine huts. After a few days Anne and I had learned how to move along without getting tangled in the rope, leaving too much slack or jerking the climber ahead, things many pure rock climbers never learn as they are apt to move one at a time.

It was a wind-still day on top of Les Diablerets and we ate our bread and cheese with a semicircular view of the alpine giants: Mt. Blanc just over the French border and the great peaks of the Oberland and the Valais whose snowfields and glaciers were all glistening white. To me it was a vision of the Promised Land.

Then what intense pleasure it was to come down off the sunbaked cliffs to the first alp, or mountain pasture, and drink great gulps of ice cold water from streams flowing through meadows of green grass and flowers. There were dark blue gentians, anemones, white and pink saxifrage with small yellow centers, and most beautiful of all, the alpenroses.

There would be cows and goats grazing, many wearing bells of different tones that made lovely music as they moved along. I envied the cheese makers who summered with their flocks, rarely leaving their picturesque, weatherbeaten huts in the high, cool uplands to go down to the hot valleys.

We spent our last night in a mountain inn, a bit more than a hut but less than a hotel, where we ate six-egg omelets and drank quarts of warm milk, fresh from a herd of Brown Swiss cows. There was a piano and we stretched out on the floor after dinner while Hassler Whitney, who is a talented musician as well as mathematician and mountain climber, played many of the Bach fugues from memory with hardly a false note, a performance all the more remarkable as his fingers had been handling a climbing rope, or been curled around an ice axe, all that day.

The innkeeper brought out bottles of wine and by midnight we had formulated plans for the next few weeks. My sister Anne decided to join a school friend in Paris; I, with the memory of that threesome setting forth for unbeknown adventures from Montenvers still clear in my mind, chose to stay in the mountains especially as our destination was to be Chamonix.

We traveled directly to Montenvers: the two Whitney boys, Bradley Gilman and myself. I came this time, not as a tourist, but as a mountaineer proudly equipped with a rucksack, ice axe and crampons. I looked with scorn at the "trippers" on the terrace who were following Mark Twain's recipe for climbing: "Hotel veranda! Bottle of whiskey! Telescope!"

The solid Chamonix granite that we found on l'Aiguille de l'M delighted us and we resolved that the Grepon would be next. I reread Mummery's light-hearted account of his first ascent with the guides Burgener and Venez and amused myself by trying to estimate the number of alcoholic drinks they consumed during the climb. The text was full of references such as "libations should be duly poured . . .; having restored our spirits by a quiet consideration of a certain flask"; and, on the summit, they opened a bottle of champagne. Mummery comments, "it has been frequently noted that all mountains appear to be doomed to pass through three stages: an inaccessible peak--The most difficult ascent in the Alps--An easy day for a lady."

The Grepon was not really I thought, "an easy day for a lady." I had climbed harder pitches on Ragged Mt. and other cliffs in Connecticut, but the exposure was awesome on most of the traverse of the narrow, crenelated ridge and this made all the difference. The route is largely hidden from below and the climber has a series of delightful surprises as he discovers the flaws in the mountain's defenses.

A couple of days later we headed for the Grand Charmoz and had the misfortune of following an Englishman sandwiched between two guides whose idea was to reach the top as soon as possible.

The unfortunate client was poked with an ice axe from below and hauled from above like a piece of baggage until he was reduced to exhaustion and tears. No sooner on top, the two guides (who looked very much like gangsters) prepared a rappel for the descent. To my suggestion that they give their client a rest one replied "Foutez moi la paix" (roughly translated, "Mind your own business") and lowered their unhappy Englishman off the summit tower.

It was early in the day, a fine one, and we lazed on the summit rocks, ate bread, cheese and chocolate and admired the view of the great Chamonix aiguilles. Hassler had his head buried in the "Guide Vallot," which gave detailed descriptions of the various routes. He suggested that rather than returning the way we had come, we do the traverse, a much more demanding climb. I seconded the motion but Roger and Brad were meeting friends in Chamonix and had to hurry down. So we parted company, each party taking one rope.

"Hass" and I had a delightful climb on the slabs that formed the broken arete of the Charmoz, stopping often to consult the guide book. We then, as directed, headed down the steep face which involved several long rappels. Our single rope was barely long enough and I was soon in trouble; first to go down, I found myself at the end of the rope, hanging against a sheer rock wall. There was no way I could climb back up the rope so, remembering our maneuvers on the Mt. Carmel cliffs, I started swinging back and forth in ever widening arcs until I was directly above a ledge a few feet below me. I took a chance--I had to--and jumped, landing on the ledge and keeping my balance.

As soon as I stopped shaking (the tension and effort had been great) I called up to Hass, who was out of sight but could hear me, to move the rappel point till it was directly above me. He did so and joined me with no difficulty on the correct route that had been hidden from above and now seemed obvious when seen from below. We hurried on down to the glacier and rested, eating our one can of sardines washed down with sips of melting snow water. This was our last climb as a storm boiled up from the south, coating the mountains with a layer of snow and ice.

The next two summers my only climbs were on eastern cliffs, ranging as far north as the White Mountains, as far south as West Virginia. New friends included Tom Rawles, an instructor at Yale, Bill Willcox, a Yale graduate student (presently editing the Franklin Papers) and his brother Alan, a New York lawyer.

They proposed a climbing holiday in Zermatt and I jumped at the chance. I should mention that these weekend trips and this trip to Europe were possible as I had a small, independent income that permitted me to travel as I pleased, within reason.

We met in Zermatt in July, 1931. Although I had seen many photographs and paintings of the Matterhorn, they hadn't prepared me for the reality: "a pointed mountain, pointing at the stars, looming up above its white encircling glaciers, dark and beautiful."

We dined formally our first evening at the Monte Rosa, our hotel, the men in dinner jackets, I in a dinner dress, as such was the custom set by the chiefly British climbers who headquartered there. Dinner over, we adjoined to a large living room for coffee and were joined by Bernhardt Biner who was to be our guide.

Bernhardt was blue eyed and blond, tall, and well built, who spoke with an English accent, because, as he told us, he had spent a year in England. He was the "chef des Guides" in Zermatt and our visit was interrupted when another guide hurried in and asked what to do about two guideless Germans stuck high up on the Matterhorn. Bernhardt gave the guide instructions in German and then turned his attention back to us, confiding to me that "he was not the best guide in Zermatt, but was the best lady's guide," an opinion I was never to dispute.

For training we started on the Untergabelhorn, an easy climb but involving a lot of height difference. Part way up we found an Australian lying on the turf and groaning. He explained that he climbed as fast as he could, "till I become bloody sick," and "No, I don't want any help." So we left him on his green sick bed, reached the top and descended in a downpour that lasted a week, piling up new snow on the peaks.

It cleared one day, as it does, and after several days climbing on the Riffelhorn and on boulders north of town we walked up to the Trift Hotel to sleep before climbing the Obergabelhorn. On the descent from this peak I had my first experience with an avalanche. It was a hot afternoon as we worked our way, rather tediously, down unstable scree slopes.

Bernhardt spotted a long steep snow gully that he thought might afford a quick route to the valley below. He anchored himself on the edge of the couloir and payed out rope as I climbed down into it. The snow was wet and I sank in to my waist.

"I don't like this" I called out to Bernhardt who was now out of sight. "Keep going till you reach the middle and then head straight down," he answered. I struggled on till suddenly, without a sound, the top layer of snow avalanched, taking me with it. A few seconds later there was a tremendous jerk, and I hung onto the rope, fighting for breath through the snow that was still pouring down from above. The avalanche ran its course and I was safe but angry. Bernhardt called down "Too dangerous," an opinion that I fervently agreed with as I climbed back up and out of the gully. This incident left me with a lasting respect for steep, wet, snow slopes.

That night, over coffee, we held a council of war. Bernhardt proposed a snow climb and suggested Monte Rosa from the Italian side, a steep 8,000-foot crescent-shaped face comparable to the Brenva face of Mt. Blanc.

This face is bisected by the Marinelli Couloir, into which most of the falling rock and ice from the upper section of the mountain finds its way. The first man to climb this face, a guide, was killed repeating his route as he was bivouacking near the edge of the Marinelli. The Italian Alpine Club now has a hut at an elevation of approximately 10,000 feet and we would sleep there the night before our climb.

We took on another guide, Hugo Lehner, and left by train for Domodossala, then transferring to an ancient Fiat for the drive to Macugnaga, the village nearest the base of our peak. There we left the car and hiked up the dusty trail in the broiling Italian sun to the Belvedere Hut, or Inn where we arrived perspiring freely. The grass was soon littered with damp socks, shirts and alpinists. A rustic meal followed, with fowls wading in the soup, roosters pecking at our bare toes and a large and unusually hairless pink sow watching us with her one baleful eye.

We continued after lunch and in the course of the next four hours discovered one of the most tedious and hot hut trails in the Alps. I was puzzled to see on the slopes above me what appeared to be clouds of smoke coming right up out of the rocks. As we drew near the Marinelli I saw that the source was the hut itself where we found three French boys and their guides trying to cook supper over a smoky fire in a battered iron stove. We added a pot of soup, with bits of sausage to thicken it and, with bread and cheese, this was our dinner.

Evening in the hut was not exactly cozy. When we stepped outside for a breath of fresh air the intense cold drove us back inside and we resigned ourselves to sleeping in the interior. We divided the four mattresses among the ten of us and I, at least, was tired enough to sleep soundly.

We crossed the quiet Marinelli Couloir at 3:30 the following morning, and then had two hours of easy climbing on rock. We pushed on, now over snow, and our second breakfast was on a small rock island below a steep snow slope. Almost directly above us we could see the rocks of the summit ridge that looked about three hours away. They looked closer here than they did for the next six.

Just below us we could see the other party bound for the Nordend. Beyond the sea of cloud that covered the Italian plain, were the Ortler, Cresta Agutza and other distant peaks silhouetted against the sun and glowing with marvelous colors. In the foreground the tops of the peaks loomed up through the clouds like black islands floating in a misty Aegean sea.

We strapped on our crampons and climbed steep snow slopes between the Marinelli that we wanted to avoid, and the ice fall on our left. This slope finally merged into the couloir and forced us to find our way up through the seracs that finally barred our way effectively. The tension increased almost unbearably, for me at least, as we hurried across the Marinelli to reach the base of a rudimentary rock ridge. At the top of the rib we had another rest and watched avalanches of flour-like snow pour off the terraced cliffs of the Nordend.

The sun was now hot and the first rocks were beginning to shoot down the couloir, about a hundred yards wide here, with a horrid, whining sound. We crossed it for the last time, slowly because of the steep angle of the slope and the wet snow sticking to our crampons, trying to ignore the stones that were now coming down almost continuously. Safe on the far side, I watched Bill and Alan, on the second rope, dive for the shelter of a small crevasse just off the couloir to escape a shower of large rocks that just missed them. Although the main stone fall was down the Marinelli chute, we were exposed to some stones from above for the next three hours with only one protected spot, behind a big serac where we took another rest.

The fresh snow on the route was wet and formed great balls on the bottom of each crampon and climbing was exhausting work. I would drive my ice axe in as far as I could reach and pull myself up with my arms. The bergschrund, where the snow and ice breaks away from the underlying rock leaving a crevasse-like chasm, was in this case a hundred meters or so below the rocks of the summit ridge and filled with snow. We crossed it easily and above was the only ice slope we found on the whole face.

We climbed to some small rocks projecting through the snow, anchored ourselves and tried to ignore the rocks that were whizzing down for the half hour it took Bernhardt to cut steps up to the cliffs of the summit ridge. We had joined both ropes together and with this protection were able to hurry up the steps to Bernhardt who was belaying us from his rocky perch.

It was a tremendous relief to finally be out of the line of fire. Without helmets, or protection of any kind, it was a helpless feeling and the danger had lasted for many hours. I am sure that this climb should be done earlier in the day, before the sun has had a chance to melt the snow and ice that cement the rocks in place, and turn the Marinelli into "the greatest avalanche trough in Europe."

We had our third meal of the day on a rocky perch with a spectacular view down the east face, and beyond, the green valleys of Italy. In perfect safety we watched several avalanches, some of rock, others of snow and ice, roar down the Marinelli. The larger boulders gouged great trenches in the snow leaving ugly, black streaks where they uncovered the ice beneath.

The route then led over snow and ice-covered rocks to the summit ridge and on to the Dufour Spitze, at 15,203 feet, the highest point on Monte Rosa, which we reached at 2:30, just eleven hours after crossing the Marinelli for the first time. I found slabs on the summit that were not only level, but also dry, and I stretched out in the sun, suddenly very tired and not a bit hungry.

I lay on my stomach with my chin resting on my crossed hands and looked down on the Matterhorn and the other great peaks of the Valais surrounded by their world of ice and snow. Dozing, I thought of the many who had climbed Monte Rosa since its first ascent in 1854. I had a series of dream-like images: of Winthrop Young, slowly and perhaps painfully, making his way up on the one leg left him after World War I; of Queen Margherita of Italy, with her big entourage and her two little dogs romping through the snow; of Vittorio Sella, the great Italian mountain photographer, muffled against the cold during the first winter ascent.

Bernhardt persuaded me to drink some sweet lemon-flavored tea. I was soon completely restored and we raced down to the Betemps Hut in an hour and fifteen minutes. We walked up to the Riffelberg, and caught the train down the Zermatt, all delighted we had climbed the East face and I, for one, resolved never to repeat it.

Alan and Bill Willcox, Tom Rawles and Bernhardt all came to the station to see me off as I was leaving before the rest of the group. I was relectant to leave my friends and the mountains and spent the trip down to Visp leaning out of the train window for last glimpses of the Matterhorn.

I had just settled myself in my compartment in the train for Geneva when Bernhardt came bounding in and sat down beside me. He explained that he had "business down the valley," so had hopped on his motor bike and roared down to Visp. We talked of the climbs we had done, planned future expeditions and I promised that I would return as soon as possible, preferably in winter or spring with a pair of skis.

I realize that I was very fortunate to have climbed in the days when it was possible to explore and make first ascents in reasonably accessible ranges rather than to have to travel to the "ends of the earth."

In retrospect I realize that I enjoyed the challenge of exploring unknown ranges, the route finding on unclimbed mountains and the unique sensation one has when setting foot on a virgin summit, more than pure rock climbing which is deliberate and slow. The latter takes a great deal of patience, a quality I am somewhat lacking in.

Elizabeth D. (Betty) Woolsey was born in Albuquerque, New Mexico and started her climbing career in the Sandia Mountains. Vassar educated , Betty spent a great deal of time climbing with the likes of Fritz Wiessner and Hans Kraus in many of the great mountain ranges of the world, doing first ascents in the Alps, the Tetons and the Canadian Rockies. Betty was also responsible, or at least partly so, for the refinement of ski mountaineering in the Alps. She was a member and captain of the American Women's ski team from 1937 to 1940.